I0480069

CONTEMPORARY ART

FROM CRESCENT MOON PUBLISHING

The Art of Andy Goldsworthy
by William Malpas

The Art of Andy Goldsworthy
by William Malpas

Andy Goldsworthy: Touching Nature
by William Malpas

Andy Goldsworthy In Close-Up
by William Malpas

The Art of Richard Long
by William Malpas

Constantin Brancusi: Sculpting the Essence of Things
by James Pearson

Alison Wilding: The Embrace of Sculpture
by Susan Quinnell

Eric Gill: Nuptials of God
by Anthony Hoyland

The Erotic Object: Sexuality in Sculpture
From Prehistory to the Present Day
by Susan Quinnell

Minimal Art and Artists in the 1960s and After
by Laura Garrard

Land Art, Earthworks, Installations, Environments, Sculpture
by William Malpas

Land Art: A Complete Guide to Landscape, Environmental,
Earthworks, Nature, Sculpture and Installation Art
by William Malpas

Richard Long In Close-Up
by William Malpas

Land Art In Close-Up
by William Malpas

Colourfield Painting: Minimal, Cool, Hard Edge, Serial
and Post-Painterly Abstract Art From the Sixties to the Present
by Laura Garrard

Mark Rothko: The Art of Transcendence
by Julia Davis

FRANK STELLA

FRANK STELLA

American Abstract Artist

James Pearson

CRESCENT MOON

CRESCENT MOON PUBLISHING
P.O. Box 393
Maidstone
Kent, ME14 5XU
United Kingdom

First published 1994. Fourth edition 2011.
© James Pearson 2011.

Printed and bound in the U.S.A.
Set in Book Antiqua 10 on 13pt.
Designed by Radiance Graphics.

British Library Cataloguing in Publication data

Pearson, James
Frank Stella: American Abstract Artist. – 3rd ed. – (Painters Series)
1. Stella, Frank – criticism and interpretation 2. Painting, Modern –
20th century – United States 3. Painting, American
I. Title
759.1'3

ISBN-13 9781861713162 (Pbk)

ISBN-13 9781861713179 (Hbk)

Contents

Acknowledgements

Ameringer & Yohe Fine Art, New York, Matthew Marks Gallery, New York, and Harry N. Abrams, publishers, New York and London.

Thanks to the authors quoted and their publishers, and to copyright owners of the illustrations.

Exciting abstract expressionist painting seemed to be everywhere. I went from gallery to gallery, museum to museum, opening to opening, and then back to my studio to look at my own painting... What seems to me now to be special about my experience in New York in the late fifties is this sense of literal pictorial support. The painting activity surrounding me held me up physically and emotionally. The painting activity that was flowering everywhere was very open and available.

Frank Stella, *Working Space*

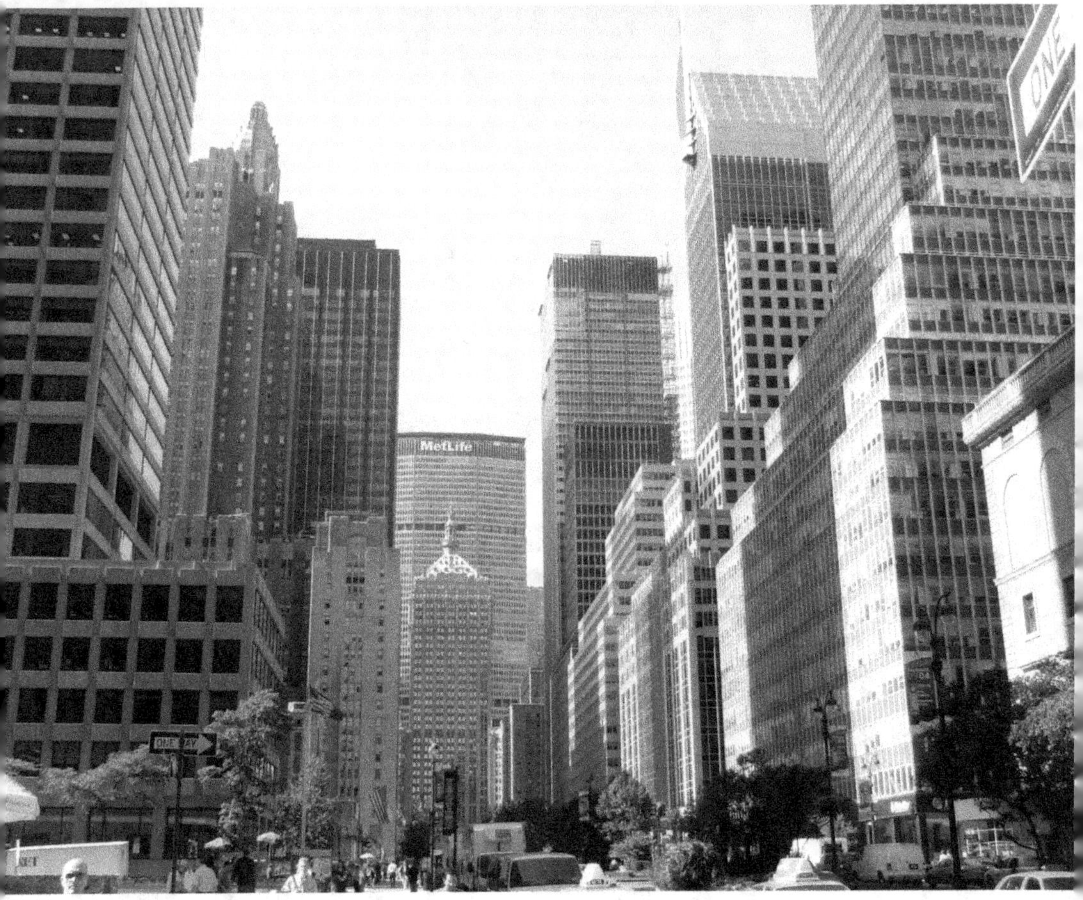

Frank Stella's home town, New York City, the centre of contemporary American art

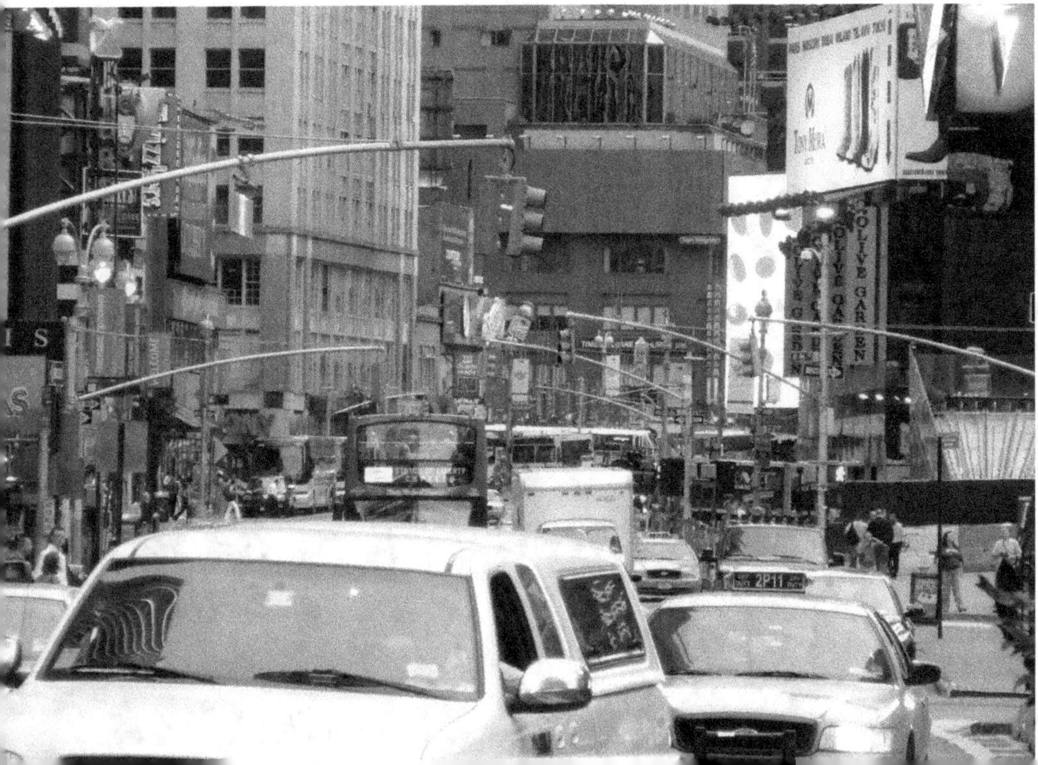

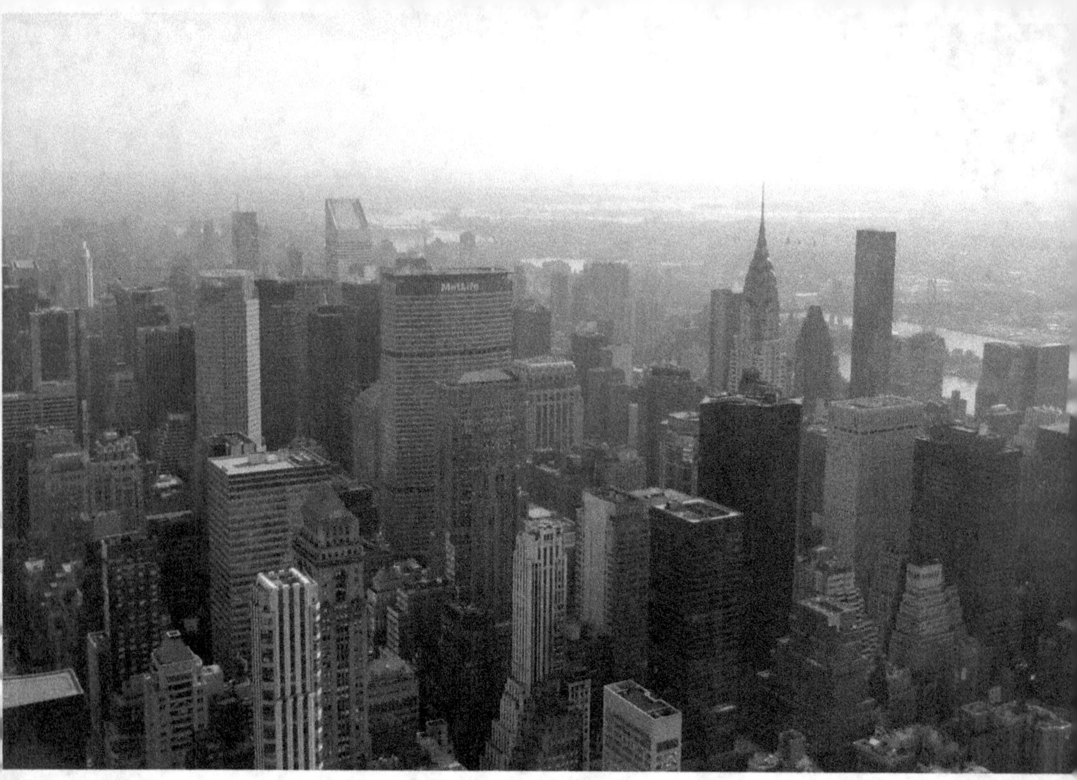
MetLife

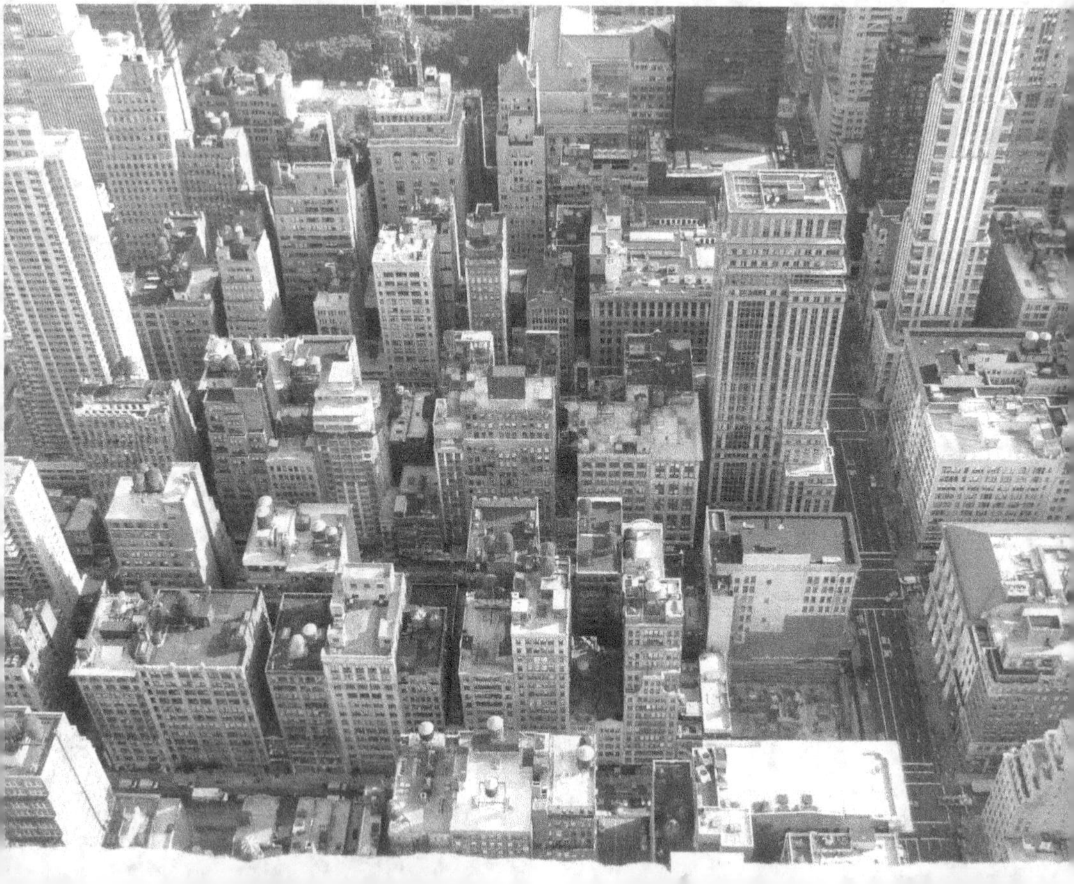

1

Influences and Tradition

Take, as an example, the first printed criticism of my work, which appeared in the New Yorker in 1960. There Robert Coates lamented "how sad it was to see the 23-year-old Frank Stella right back where Mondrian was twenty-five years ago." I realized that this remark was a polite put-down; nevertheless, the thrill it gave me was overpowering. It would have been an honour to be right back where Mondrian was twenty-five years ago, if that had been the case; but even without that possibility, the fact that my name appeared in print in the same sentence with Mondrian's seemed to be an incredible affirmation of personality and ability. It actually took me a while to get over the shock of publicity, the quick glare of history passing over me.

Frank Stella, *Working Space* (146)

Frank Stella was born on May 12, 1936 in Malden, MA. He studied at the Phillips Academy, Prince University. In 1958 he moved to New York City, where he has lived ever since. He married critic Barbara Rose in 1961; his second wife was Harriet McGurk; he has 5 children. Stella has had many important one-man shows and retrospectives (at Gotham's MOMA in 1970 and 1987, for example), taken part in key group shows (such as *Sixteen Americans, The Shaped Canvas, Systematic Painting*), designed dance costumes and sets (in 1967, for Merce Cunningham), painted a BMW (an 'art car', 1976), and lectured at Harvard University (1984). Stella has had many awards, including the National Medal of Arts (2009), which he received from US President Barack Obama.

I'd seen Frank Stella's art in England at the Tate Gallery (which has one or two pieces), in the late 1970s, but it was the London show of June and July, 1985, which really brought home the impact and beauty of Stella's later painting-as-sculpture works.

Frank Stella knows where he fits into the history of contemporary art: he comes after Barnett Newman and is contemporary with Jasper Johns (b. 1930), Jim Dine (b. 1935) and Sol LeWitt (b. 1928). Stella writes thus of Barnett Newman, and of Morris Louis in *Working Space*:

> The strength of his [Newman's] painting comes from the ability of the stripes (or, as he liked to call them, "zips") to attach themselves to and into the background. They fit beautifully, zipping the space together. Newman sets up the motion of his figuration counter to the motion of the space supporting it... It may be that what makes Morris Louis's late paintings so appealing is their peculiar Kandinsky-like understanding of Newman. Louis brought a determined looseness to Newman's abstraction that Kandinsky would have applauded. Louis had the opportune sense of contiguous touch that is so necessary to link the moving elements of abstraction. This touch enabled him to exploit separation in a way that modern painting admires but cannot seem to imitate. (Working Space, hereafter abbreviated to WS, 123-125)

At the same time, Frank Stella's art broke with earlier art, as Mel Bochner noted:

> Stella's work neatly bypassed most of the traits common to the painting that preceded him. Subsequent art, therefore, did not have to be the same as previous art.[1]

In *Working Space*, Frank Stella nostalgically recalled his early

1 Mel Bochner, 1966, 40

days in New York, the great metropolis that was the centre of art in America (as it still is – but now it's the capital of the global art industry), where he arrived as a young would-be artist.

> *Exciting abstract expressionist painting seemed to be everywhere. I went from gallery to gallery, museum to museum, opening to opening, and then back to my studio to look at my own painting... The painting activity surrounding me held me up physically and emotionally. The painting activity that was flowering everywhere was very open and available...* (WS, 153)

Donald Judd often praised Frank Stella. Getting rid of illusion in painting, Judd said, was one of the 'decisive advances' made by Stella and Kenneth Noland (1962, 51). Stella's new sense of space, Judd argued, 'makes Abstract Expressionism seem now an inadequate style, makes it appear a compromise with representational art and its meaning.'[2] For Judd, a Stella painting (referring to one of the aluminium series) was 'something of an object, it is a single thing, not a field with something in it, and it has almost no space'.[3]

Sheldon Nodelman concurred with Donald Judd, claiming that Frank Stella and Kenneth Noland had finally done away with illusionism (1967, 77). Willis Domingo said that Stella solved 'the contradiction in a spatial ambiguity whereby literal and illusionistic space become indistinguishable from one another' (W. Domingo, 44-45).

The holistic quality of Abstract Expressionism was crucial – the instantaneous Zen-like 'all-over effect', as Barnett Newman described it. Donald Judd said that this holistic approach was the legacy of Jackson Pollock: this unification was 'the paramount quality and scheme of Abstract Expressionism', and it is central to the art of Stella, as well as Kenneth Noland, John Chamberlain,

---

2 D. Judd, 1964, 28, in *Complete Writings 1959-1975*, 150
3 D. Judd, 1963, 55

Mark Rothko and Barnett Newman.[4] In "Specific Objects", Judd wrote that

> it isn't necessary for a work to have a lot of things to look at, to compare, to analyze one by one, to contemplate. The thing as a whole, its qualities as a whole, is what is interesting.[5]

Jackson Pollock and Abstract Expressionism had to come first before Frank Stella's paintings could blossom. Stella makes many references to Pollock in *Working Space*:

> we need to use Pollock. We see the potential: in the speed of the moving line, in the encapsulation and entanglement of shallow space, and in the sheer beauty of the painting's literalness, what amounts to the embodiment of its abstraction... We should be able to expand Pollock's pictorial space and to follow the lead of his paint skeins. Painting desperately needs the literalness, immediacy, freedom, and clarity of the drip paintings. (60)

Jasper Johns' ideas on painting are much more romantic than Frank Stella's: Johns writes of his desires for painting:

> I think that one wants from a painting a sense of life. The final suggestion, the final statement, has to be not a deliberate statement but a helpless statement. It has to be what you can't avoid saying.[6]

When one looks at Frank Stella's paintings, the intention is that one sees all of the painting at once. The effect really is like that of Zen Buddhism, and the references to Zen of course were occurring in places such as the Beat poets in New York in the late 1950s, when Stella was starting out as a painter. The Beat poets – Allen Ginsburg, Jack Kerouac, William Burroughs, *et al*, appropriated Oriental philosophy for their own ends. They

---

4 D. Judd, 1964, 28, in *Complete Writings 1959-1975*, 151
5 D. Judd: "Specific Objects", in Gerd de Vries, ed: *On Art: Artists' Writings on the Changed Notion of Art After 1965*, Cologne 1974, 128
6 J. Johns, quoted in David Sylvester: "Interview", *Jasper Johns Drawings*, Museum of Modern Art, Oxford 1974, 14

Americanized it, one might say.

Frank Stella steers clear of such philosophizing, but the all-over, instantaneous effect he desired in painting has much in common with the 'timeless now' of Taoist and Zen philosophy. It is other American painters who theorized in the grand fashion, bringing in Oriental mysticism – such as Robert Motherwell and Barnett Newman. In *Working Space*, Stella sticks to theorizing in the Western tradition about æsthetics, making references to the 'great' names of Western painting: Titian, Michelangelo Merisi de Caravaggio, Pablo Picasso and Peter Rubens.

Frank Stella relates to the Old Masters and historical tradition. Just as Kasimir Malevich made references to the Byzantine ikons tradition and Brice Marden acknowledges Old Masters such as the Spanish painters Francisco de Zurbarán and Diego Velásquez, and Édouard Manet and Paul Cézanne, so Stella refers consciously to many former artists. Michael Fried, in a "New York Letter' of 1964, writes that Frank Stella and Barnett Newman are 'historically self-aware'.[7] Stella's acute (art) historical self-awareness came out very clearly in his book *Working Space*.

---

7 Michael Fried, 1964, 59

2

Frank Stella's Paintings

Frank Stella's paintings, like all paintings, demand that one see them in the flesh, so to speak. To look at a Frank Stella painting (early or late) in a black-and-white *or colour* reproduction in a book wholly misses the point. The colours, shapes, patterns, forms, canvases, stretchers and scale of his paintings are so powerful, one has to see them close up. Not in any form of reproduction. His paintings are very physical paintings, as all paintings are, of course. This is obvious, but it's no good discussing Stella without first getting close to his paintings. This is true also of Berthe Morisot, Artemisa Gentileschi, Diego Velásquez, Mark Rothko, Anselm Keifer, Giotto, or any painter one cares to name. Although Stella's late works still retain a frontal aspect, one can walk around the sides and look at them from other directions. The late works are opened out, with slabs of aluminium tilted and curving away from the gallery wall.

To grasp Frank Stella's art, then, one needs this 3-D view,

because the interrelations of the parts of metal and paint are complex. Stella's copper and aluminium metallic paint canvases too are complicated spatially and physically. Some of the 1960s copper and aluminium stripe paintings are vast, zigzagging down gallery walls. Paintings such as *D* are a seven-foot polygon which, because of its scale, as with the large-scale works of Mark Rothko, Morris Louis, Barnett Newman, Franz Kline or Willem de Kooning, towers over the spectator. Even so, Stella's works are not domineering in the way that Rothko or Reinhardt or Motherwell can be. The very lightness and bright colours of Stella's art dispel the sense of being overwhelmed by the paintings. Stella's art is not oppressive or gloomy at all, but is vivacious, muscular, positive and sometimes joyous.

Frank Stella's paintings command relatively high prices in the art market, though perhaps not as high as Jasper Johns' or Mark Rothko's works. In Stella's 1987 show at Knoedler Gallery in London's Cork Street, the larger pieces were selling for 260,000 dollars. His art was derisorily called 'bank art', the sort big companies buy. Stella has always been successful and popular, it seems. He has not gone 'out of fashion': his works have been a part of group shows and one-person shows ever since the late fifties/ early sixties. His Charles Eliot Norton lectures in 1983-84 at Harvard University were very popular with students.

Among Frank Stella's more recent shows and projects are exhibitions at the Metropolitan Museum of Art, *Painting Into Architecture* in 2007 (including on the roof), 'Stella Sounds' in Washington, DC (2011), and solo shows in Stockholm (2008, 2009, 2010), Belgium (2008), Germany (2007), Harvard University (2006), San Francisco (2005), Basel (2007), Dartmouth College (2010), Grand Rapids (2009), New York City (2006, 2007, 2009), Princeton (2008), London (2005, 2011) and Santiago (2005). A travelling retrospective is planned for 2014-15.

Stella has art in most of the major public collections in the U.S.

of A., and in London, Paris, Switzerland, Canada, Tokyo, Sydney, etc.

Frank Stella has carved out a niche in the art world for himself. There are no works quite like Stella's around. There are similar pieces, but Stella's works remain instantly recognisable as Stella's works. The same cannot be said for any number of other artists.

3

Frank Stella and Jasper Johns

Frank Stella was certainly influenced by Jasper Johns, as William Rubin notes:

> *Frank was, I think, very interested in Johns' work in his last months at Princeton and immediately after he graduated. Johns' flags would be the pictures we'd have to look to in that sense, because they provided a concept of a picture that would be striped, as these pictures are, and also where the stars are a kind of box, which is not unrelated to the box in the center of* Coney Island. *Johns' pictures interested Frank because of certain repetitions, repetition of numbers or letters or stripes of the flag, and Frank saw possibilities in this repetition which Johns himself was not to see.*[8]

The power of Jasper Johns' works comes partly from his incredible surfaces, which are made of oil and wax or encaustic, spread thickly on the canvas. Paintings such as *White Flag, Highway, Canvas* and *Scent* are really exquisite works, so intensely

---

8 Quoted in E. de Antonio, 138.

tactile and sumptuous.[9] In Frank Stella's art the sense of surface is not as stridently (or as self-consciuosly) sensual as in Johns. Stella is interested in different things.

Frank Stella was relatively successful early on in his career, like his contemporaries Jasper Johns and Robert Rauschenberg. These painters were popular with critics and collectors early on in their careers, giving them a boost beyond millions of other struggling artists. Of Johns' career, which parallels that of Stella, Peter Fuller writes:

> In 1958, Alfred Barr cooled his support of Abstract Expressionism, and urged artists to rebel against their elders. Significantly, Barr, too, was involved in the manufacture of Jasper Johns. Until 1958, Johns was an obscure artist who had inserted certain Dada-esque representational components into what was essentially a modified Abstract Expressionist style. That year, he was given a one-man show by Castelli; before it opened, the decision had been taken to put him on the front cover of Art News (hitherto a partisan Abstract Expressionist publication). MOMA immediately purchased examples of his work.[10]

William Rubin discussed the relation between Jasper Johns and Frank Stella, and the influence it had on Stella, in the early 1970s:

> there's a vast difference in sensibilities and in aims, so I don't want to make this relationship too close, but I think Johns also had one other importance. That is, his flag pictures and some of the other images he made were the first paintings in which the field of the pictures is absolutely identical with the motif of the picture: the boundaries of the pictures are identical with the boundaries of the flag. The flag is laid out as a flat pattern on the surface, and although Johns is a representational painter in that sense and Frank became an abstract painter, I think the notion of making the motif identical with the

9 *White Flag*, 1955, encaustic and collage on canvas, 199 x 307cm, collection: the artist; *Highway*, 1959, encaustic and collage on canvas, 190.5 x 154.9cm, collection: Mrs Leo Castelli, New York; *Scent*, 1973-4, oil and encaustic on canvas, 182.9 x 320.6cm, collection: Ludwig Aachen; *Canvas*, 1956, encaustic and collage on canvas with objects, 76.2 x 63.5cm, collection; the artist.
10 Peter Fuller: "American Painting Since Last Year", *Art Monthly*, June 1979, in David Shapiro, 178

*shape of the field, even though that shape remains rectangular in Johns'
flag, lurks somewhere behind what would become the principle of Frank's
shaped canvas. And that principle is, if I can define it in its simplest way,
essentially that the boundary of the picture is going to be determined by the
governing pattern of the surface, and that there will be an absolute
reciprocity between the outer shape of the picture, which might be
considered simply the outside line of a pattern that operates over the entire
surface.*[11]

11 W. Rubin, in E. de Antonio, 138-9

4

Stella Parallels

Contemporary with Frank Stella's paintings in the 1960s was Samuel Beckett's exploration of self-referential art. Stella in *Working Space* emphasizes his roots in modernism, as well the Old Masters, and Beckett is one of the major modernists (like James Joyce, T.S. Eliot, Gertrude Stein, Marcel Proust and D.H. Lawrence). Starting from the statement that there is 'nothing to express' and 'nothing with which to express', Beckett wrote short, condensed pieces which he called 'fizzles', which have similarities with Stella's smooth surfaces, and with the negation of Ad Reinhardt's *Black Paintings*. Beckett reduced fictions to a series of words, much as Stella reduced paintings to simply paint on canvas. In Beckett and Stella the actuality of the materials of their art is crucial. Stella's credo – what you see is what you get – is echoed by Beckett. Disliking discussing his art, Beckett insisted on the texts themselves, which needed no glosses to make them explicit. Likewise, Stella insists on the physicality of his painting, and there is no need for explanations. Of Beckett, Stella said:

> *The idea of repetition appealed to me, and there were certain literary things that were in the air that corresponded to it. At the time I was going to school, Samuel Beckett was very popular. Beckett is pretty lean, you might say, but he is also slightly repetitive to me in the sense that certain very simple situations in which not much happened are a lot like repetition. I don't know, it struck me that bands, repeated bands would be somewhat more like a Beckett-like situation than, say, a big, blank canvas... There was something Beckett did that seemed kind of insistent about what little was there. It also seemed to fit me.* (E. de Antonio, 141)

Samuel Beckett's short fictions *Ping, Lessness, Imagination Dead Imagine, All Strange Away* a n d *Still,* with their mathematical descriptions of boxes, rotundas and cylinders, seem to be poetic equivalents of the smooth, rigid volumes of Minimalism (Donald Judd, Robert Morris, Carl Andre and Dan Flavin).

This is an extract from *Still* (1975), a superbly poetic text, and about the most tranquil in all of Samuel Beckett's *œuvre*:

> *Bright at last close of a dark day the sun shines out at last and goes down. Sitting quite still at valley window normally turn head now and see it the sun low in the southwest sinking. Even get up certain moods and go stand by western window quite still watching it sink and then the afterglow. Always quite still some reason some time past this hour at open window facing south in small upright wicker chair with armrests. Eyes stare out unseeing till first movement some time past close though unseeing still while still light.* (1984, 183)

And from *Ping,* an evocation a white body in a white space:

> *Given rose only just bare white body fixed one yard white on white invisible. All white all known murmurs only just almost never always the same all known. Light heat hands hanging palms front white on white invisible. Bare white body fixed ping elsewhere.*

And this is from a late Samuel Beckett work, 1983's *Worstward*

Ho, with evocations of nothingness and void, and a steady descent into darkness – always with the fading light in Beckett's writing:

> *Worsening words whose unknown. Whence unknown. At all costs unknown. Now for to say as worst they may only they only they. Dim void shades all they. Nothing save what they say. Somehow say. Nothing save they. What they say. Whosoever whence-soever say. As worst they may fail worse to say.*
>
> •
>
> *So leastward on. So long as dim still. Dim undimmed. Or dimmed to dimmer still. To dimmost dim. Leastmost in dimmost dim. Utmost dim. Leastmost in utmost dim. Unworsenable dim.* (1992, 29, 33)

Like Frank Stella, Samuel Beckett often employed the Minimalists' use of seriality, of doing one thing then another, in sequence. Artists such as Brice Marden, Sol LeWitt, Donald Judd and Carl Andre based some of their artworks on series of numbers or patterns. Minimal ethics can produce some extremes of mathematics and seriality. Carl Andre's *37 Pieces of Work* is a good example of Minimal æsthetic permutations taken to extremes:

> *Taken as a whole* 37 Pieces of Work *consists of 1,296 plates, 216 each of aluminium, copper, steel, magnesium, lead and zinc. Each metal appears alone in individual six-foot square plains. Then alternates with another, checkerboard fashion, in every possible permutation. Since each of the six metals in the large piece was laid out in the alphabetical order of its chemical symbol, alternating successively with the others, there are two versions of each combination.*[12]

Like Samuel Beckett and the Minimal artists, Frank Stella moved calmly and methodically from one thing to another. Sol LeWitt (perhaps the most ascetic of the Minimal artists, for all his work is done in the planning stage), believes that Jasper Johns and other artists use numbers, but not necessarily mathematics: not just 'anyone uses mathematics *per se*', wrote LeWitt,

---

12 David Bourdon, 1978, 56. See Mel Bochner, 1967, 39-43

FRANK STELLA

*They use **numbers**. It's just like Jasper Johns using, 1, 2, 3, 4, 5, 6, 7, 8, 9, 0. I use numbers only as a way of drawing something.*[13]

---

13 Quoted in F. Colpitt, 63

5

Space, Abstraction, Aesthetics

Everyone knows that the future belongs to surface and color, self-generating and self-sustaining abstractions bound together in an undeniable presence that makes itself felt as art. Everyone knows that illusionism gets in the way of an uncluttered, pure expression of surface and colour.

Frank Stella, *Working Space* (97)

In *Working Space*, Frank Stella sets out his interpretation of 20th century painting, and abstraction in particular. There is a crisis in abstract painting, Stella says, which is similar to the crisis facing painting in the post-Renaissance era (WS, 1f). Abstraction has to find a 'new kind of pictoriality', to go beyond the achievements of the abstract modernists. Stella, though, regards abstraction very highly, saying that abstraction forms 'the core of our thinking of how painting should be conceived and understood' (WS, 110). Stella cites the usual figures of 20th century abstraction: Wassily Kandinsky, Kasimir Malevich, Pablo Picasso, Pet Mondrian, Paul Klee, Barnett Newman and Mark Rothko. Abstraction is still young, and inexperienced, Stella says. The aim, for Stella, is 'to create space – space... in which the subjects of painting can live' (WS, 5). Stella is excited about space, and talks about how painting can control and evoke, deny and displace space:

> *The balance between positive and negative is always exquisite; the displacement and redeployment of space always constitute a marvel.* (WS, 141)

Frank Stella traces, in art historical fashion, the development of painterly space from Leonardo da Vinci through Raphael Sanzio and Michelangelo Buonaroti to Michelangelo Merisi de Caravaggio, Peter Rubens, Rembrandt van Rijn and Jan Vermeer, to Édouard Manet, Paul Cézanne and Piet Mondrian. For Stella, abstract art today, in particular painterly abstraction, 'has no real pictorial space – space, for example, like that of Michelangelo Merisi de Caravaggio, Édouard Manet, Piet Mondrian, Jackson Pollock, and, surprisingly, Morris Louis' (WS, 12). What Stella wants is for abstract art to gain 'some of the solidity of Italian painting' (WS, 155). The sensuality of surfaces, of textures, of brushwork, of the artist's sense of touch, is crucial to the 'greatness' of art, as Lynda Nead writes: 'the artist's subjectivity that is registered by the brushwork and surface is sexualized. Art criticism writes sex into descriptions of paint, surface and forms' (58). Paul Gauguin wrote of the sensual primacy of painting in the familiar terms of late 19th century Baudelairean 'theory of correspondences' which was used by many poets, painters and dramatists:

> *Painting is the most beautiful of all arts. In it, all sensations are condensed... A complete art which sums up all the others and completes them. – Like music, it acts on the soul through the intermediary senses: harmonious colours correspond to the harmonies of sounds.*[14]

For Frank Stella, though, abstract art isn't automatically erotic:

14 P. Gauguin: "Notes Synthetiques", in *Paul Gauguin: A Sketchbook*, tr Raymond Cogniat, Hammer Galleries, New York 1962, 57f

It is very hard for abstraction, or abstract figuration, to be sexy, and if it's not sexy, it's not art. Everyone knows that. (WS, 77)

The eroticism of abstract painting is obvious to those who find surfaces erotic, however. Rather, Frank Stella searches for sensuality in the notion of the 'working space' of a painting. Stella writes of the space a painting creates, and how this space can envelop the viewer, sensually:

An effective painting should present its space in such a way as to include both viewer and maker each with his own space intact. It is not that this experience should be literal; it is simply that the sense of space projected by the painting should seem expansive: expansive enough to include the viewing and the creation of that space. (WS, 9)

Other artists have spoken lovingly of the sensual nature of the canvas itself, the beauty of the art object. Maurice Denis wrote: '[t]he emotion – bitter or sweet, "literary" as the painters say – emerges from the canvas itself, a plane surface covered with colours.'[15] Frank Stella writes:

Painting is always face forward, always reverse or back side to painting. Bad paintings (that is, paintings that are less than they should be) are bland and dark on the reverse, while good paintings pull themselves mirac-ulously inside out to ensure their forward-looking presence as we imagine ourselves moving around them. Good paintings always seem to face the viewer, turning effortlessly as we try to slip behind them to test their illusionism. (WS, 28)

For Frank Stella, a good painting is one which creates a world, a world which involves the viewer. The edge of the painting must not be the true edge of the painting. That is, the painting must extend well beyond the painting. ('Clearly, abstraction has to move; it has to extend itself.' WS, 143) For Stella, the edge of the painting may be 'hard', as in the 'hard edge' painting of the

15 Maurice Denis: "Definitions of neotraditionism", 1890, in *Theories: 1890-1910*, Rouart et Watelin, Paris 1920, 5f

Sixties, but it must enable expansion beyond:

> *What painting wants more than anything else is working space – space to grow with and expand into, pictorial space that is capable of direction and movement, pictorial space that encourages unlimited orientation and extension. Painting does not want to be confined by boundaries of edge and surface.* (WS, 35)

A sense of space is crucial for Jasper Johns too. 'As well as I can tell,' Johns says, 'I am concerned with space. With some idea about space. And then as soon as you break space, then you have things.'[16]

For Frank Stella, the sense of space (meaning a contemporary sense of space) is still firmly caught in the Renaissance. Westerners still see the world through boxes, says Stella:

> *We are so conditioned by the window of perspective that we stand motionless in front of it, waiting for painting to organize itself according to our acquired habits... Today, although we claim to be free of the bounds of perspective, we hold slavishly to a notion of a box view of a whole... to put it another way, the flatness of abstraction today, its sense of surface... is simply the forwardmost plane, the windowed picture plane of the fifteenth century perspectival box.* (WS, 51)

What abstract art has to do, says Frank Stella, is to break out of this 15th century boxlike perspective. Western audiences are so conservative that even 'a mobile viewpoint seems to be an anathema' (WS, 51). In *Working Space* Stella seems to be disavowing his earlier, 1960s work, which seems to be supremely 'flat'.

Marcel Duchamp and Kurt Schwitters are usually cited as precursors of Robert Rauschenberg's and Jasper Johns' mixed media explorations. Rauschenberg and Johns rewrote the notion of painting-as-object by sticking objects onto it. Kurt Schwitters is

---

16 quoted in Peter Fuller: "Jasper Johns Interviewed", *Art Monthly*, no 18, July 1978, 12

often cited as a major exponent of multi-media formalism. Schwitters explained how he came to do it:

> *I simply could not see any reason why old streetcar tickets, driftwood, coat checks, wire and wheel parts, buttons, junk from the attic and heaps of refuse should not be used as material for paintings, any less than colours made in a factory.* (quoted in F. Roh, 133)

Frank Stella moved into three dimensions in the 1970s, building his paintings out from the wall, with paintings such as *Warka III* and *Leblon II*.

For Frank Stella, abstraction still offers many possibilities for painters. In *Working Space* he looked back at the past of art, particularly post-Renaissance art; but he knew that the future of painting must build on the example of Jackson Pollock.

6

Stripes, Vs, Flatness

For me, speculating about abstraction serves the purpose of explaining contradictory feelings. It explains why I love and embrace abstraction on a practical, performing level, yet remain wary of it on a theoretical level. Contradictory feelings do not create a conflict for me; that is, I do not experience any special anxiety because I am trying to make abstract painting.

Frank Stella, *Working Space* (131)

Frank Stella's sense of colour and abstraction stems largely from Northern European painting (WS, 134). Like Robert Rosenblum in his influential book *Modern Painting and the Northern Romantic Tradition*, Stella sees the Northern European painters as being the precursors of modern abstraction, and the masters of modern abstract art – Piet Mondrian, Wassily Kandinsky, Kasimir Malevich, Paul Klee – are distinctly Northern European figures. Stella's penchant for Northern Europe is apparent in this passage from *Working Space* on the Impressionists' sense of light. Though many people exalt the Impressionists, Stella reckons their light was disappointing:

*Compared with seventeenth-century Dutch painting, the light of Impress-
ionism is murky and opaque. I know this assertion will provoke argument,
but in fact Impressionism generates very little light or color through
reflection; it relies on a necessarily blunted exterior illumination and
optical mixing for most of its effects. The thin glaze technique of the north
helps to build a glassy outdoor clarity which is to be prized. It depends on a
translucent, "see-through" relationship which is the opposite of Impressionism's opaque "see-together" juxtapositions.* (WS, 145)

One can see Frank Stella striving after translucent colour and
light in his paintings, a sense of colour which will not be
'opaque', but open.

One of Jasper Johns' key statements is:

*Take an object
Do something to it
Do something else to it
" " " " "*[17]

Frank Stella took up the notion of seriality and repetition, as did
so many other artists in the 1960s, and explored it. Stella
employed simple geometric shapes in the 1960s upon which he
painted complex sequences of colours. These paintings, including
the *Protractor* series, used the simple form in order to explore other
aspects of painting. For Jasper Johns the aim was to create 'things
which are seen and not looked at', and explained further:

*Using the design of the American flag took care of a great deal for me
because I didn't have to design it. So I went on to similar things like the
targets – things the mind already knows. That gave me room to work on
other levels.*[18]

Frank Stella employed hard-edged, angular motifs, shapes such

17 Jasper Johns: "Sketchbook Notes", in *Art and Literature*, 4, Lausanne,
Spring 1965, 192
18 in Leo Steinberg: "Jasper Johns: The First Seven Years of His Art", in
Other Criteria: Confrontations with Twentieth-Century Art, Oxford University Press, New York 1972, 31

as Vs, Hs, Zs, 'notched Vs', squares and rectangles. He also used symmetry, an exact symmetry made explicit and bold by his stripes and the shaped stretchers, so that the stripe pattern, writes John Coplans, 'begins at the center and spreads outward by his use of various kinds of symmetry' ("Serial Imagery", 37). Stella wrote:

> Ken Noland has put things in the center and I'll use a symmetrical pattern, but we use symmetry in a different way. It's non-relational. In the newer American paintings we strive to get the thing in the middle, and symmetrical but just to get a kind of force, just to get the thing on the canvas. The balance factor isn't important. We're not trying to jockey everything around. (in B. Glaser, 55)

For Frank Stella, this sense of symmetry was not sited within an illusionistic space; rather, the use of hard edges, symmetry and the monochrome bands helped to push away illusionistic space:

> A symmetrical image or configuration placed on an open ground is not balanced out in the illusionistic space. The solution I arrived at – and there are probably others although I know of only one, color density – forces illusionistic space out of the painting at a constant rate by using a regulated pattern. (B. Rose, "ABC Art", 59)

Frank Stella's symmetry, then, is not concerned with 'illusionistic space', as he calls it, the space of traditional Western, post-Renaissance art, but with a new flatness. Stella said:

> I had to do something about relational painting, i.e. the balancing of the various parts of the painting with and against each other. The obvious answer was symmetry – make it the same all over.[19]

Even when the stretchers are not shaped, as in with the *Black Paintings*, which were (usually) rectangular, the V-shapes still deny illusionistic space. At first, the *Black Paintings* seem to be somewhat 'traditional', as they employ the rectangular shape.

19 F. Stella: "The Pratt Lecture", 1960, in Richardson, 1976, 78

Inside the field of the rectangle, though, Frank Stella paints, directly onto the canvas, stripes of black, in V-shapes and rect- angles, as in *Tomlinson Court Park* and *Point of Pines*.

Max Kozloff wrote of Jasper Johns' motifs, the flags and targets in "Pop Culture, Metaphysical Designs and the New Vulgarians", saying they were

> *merely so many abstract forms upon which social usage has conferred meaning, but which now, displaced into their new context, cease to function socially. From this tremendous insight alone have sprung the momentum of Pop Art and the huge quantities of abstraction that is emblematic in character.* (1962, 34-36)

The key to Jasper Johns' reworking of formalism and abstraction in the flags, targets, numbers and alphabets was precisely the sensuality of his art. It was the way he so powerfully employed the techniques of the 'Old Masters', of 'great art', that made his flags and targets so successful. For critics could not see Johns' banal signs culled from popular culture as trivial art, for Johns used one of the key elements in 'high art', the sensual, heavily impastoed surface. Johns' art could not be dismissed by critics, then as now, because its surface is as sensual and painterly as Rembrandt, Velásquez, Manet or Titian. In *Working Space*, Stella discusses Caravaggio's art:

> *The second miracle of Caravaggio is the miracle of surface. Skin, flesh, and pigment blend into reality. Painting is acknowledged as an act and as a physical fact, but immediately afterward, almost simultaneously, the presence of the human figure is felt as real, touchably there.* (11)

Frank Stella, though he would deny it, also created sensual art objects. Stella often denies any 'emotion' or 'feeling' in his art. It is not about that, he says. For some people, he knows, his art comes across as cold. Brian O'Doherty called Stella 'the Cézanne of nihilism, the master of *ennui*' (21). Donald Kuspit dubbed his art 'authoritarian' and mechanistic ("Authoritarian Abstraction", 1977, 25). He reckons his *Black Paintings* were as emotional as Mark Rothko's tragic canvases:

> *Certainly no one would see the black paintings now as cold and calculating or very logical, but they seemed to seem that way in the context of '59 and '60. They were lean compared with some paintings, but the general look of them, if you really looked, seemed to me to have an awful lot to do with somebody like Rothko in feeling – and no one accused Rothko of being cold and intellectual.* (E. de Antonio, 144)

The post-painterly, post-Abstract Expressionist painters – Ellsworth Kelly, Kenneth Noland, Richard Diebenkorn, Morris Louis, Ad Reinhardt – are regarded by some critics as having squeezed out the emotion from painting: they took the Abstract Expressionist forms and made them unexpressive. Lawrence Alloway writes:

> *If we compare paintings by Frank Stella and Ellsworth Kelly with those of the Abstract Expressionists, it becomes evident that a dimension of allusion, an aura of content, has been denied by the later artists. They certainly take off from positions given by Newman, Rothko, but the field of color, the holistic imagery, and the expanded scale of the canvas no longer imply momentous content. The allusions of older artists' feelings compared to the reduced passion of the younger generation...* (1973)

There does not seem to be much going on in Frank Stella's paintings, as in most Minimal paintings. But there is, in fact, a lot going on. Stella limits himself to a narrow set of rules. Like Brice Marden, Kenneth Noland, Barnett Newman, Morris Louis and Mark Rothko, Stella sets himself to explore a few configurations of painting. But these things – shape of the canvas, internal organization of the stripes, colour of the bands – offer up endless permutations. Painters go over the same simple patterns and set-ups again and again. Turner painted thousands of seascapes – the same basic ocean, framed in the same lower third of the picture, the same mixture of clouds and sun in the sky, and so on. Turner attacked the sky from thousands of different viewpoints and different locations, from every coastline of Britain, to France, Switzerland, Italy and Germany. Similarly, Claude Monet painted the same basic picture of a sunlit river time after time.

Like other Minimal artists, Frank Stella explored the endless permutations that a few very simple elements offered up. The results seem to be 'lean', but even in the most minimal of Minimal works there is sensuality and presence. Samuel Wagstaff notes that the Minimal painting asserts the painting above the painter: the author slips into the background: '[t]here is an attempt to suggest the presence of paint rather than the presence of the painter' (1964, 62). And Helen Frankenthaler said, like so many Sixties painters, that she didn't want the manufacture of the painting to be apparent: 'I poured the paint and used relatively few brushstrokes. I didn't want the sign of the brush or how the picture was made to appear' (in E. de Antonio, 77). Stella said that he didn't want the heroic gestures and detail of traditional or Abstract Expressionist painting:

> One could stand in front of any Abstract Expressionist work for a long time, and walk back and forth, and inspect the details of the pigment and the inflection and all the painterly brushwork for hours. But I wouldn't particularly want to do that and I also wouldn't ask anyone to do that in front of my paintings. (quoted in B. Glaser, 59)

Frank Stella's paintings are lean, but leanness does not necessarily mean unfeelingness. This is the problem that mono-chrome painting creates, and Minimal art in general. People think Minimal art is boring. In Minimal painting and sculpture, surfaces are, typically, smooth, utterly smooth and 'pure'. ('I wanted everything to be on the surface', says Stella [WS, 155]). Simplicity is exalted, as is repetition, seriality, process, flatness as well as volume and space. The many materials are flattened out and depersonalized, and gestures, so important to certain kinds of painting and sculpture (such as that of Pablo Picasso or Michelangelo Buonaroti) are suppressed. Indeed, the flatness of the surfaces, whether in the art of Robert Morris, Donald Judd, Brice Marden, Agnes Martin, Carl Andre, Ronald Bladen or Tony Smith, is crucial. But the 'boringness' of Minimal art,[20] becomes a part of the metaphysics of Minimal art, so that Lucy Lippard writes:

> *The exciting thing about... the "cool" artists is their daring challenge of the concepts of boredom, monotony and repetition... their demonstration that intensity does not have to be melodramatic.* (1966b, 50)

Certainly Frank Stella is intense: his *Black Stripe Paintings*, his *Protractor* series, his copper paintings, his *India Birds*, are intense works of art. Pieces such as *Quathlamba* (1964), *D* (1963) and *Avicenna* (1960), are very powerful paintings. *D*, in particular, is impressive: one of the *Purple Polygons* series, it is a huge (7 feet high and wide) ten-sided polygon, with the centre left empty, as so often in Stella's paintings. The exhibition of *Purple Polygons* was called 'boring' and 'monotonous' by some critics (M. Kozloff, 1964, 64; B. O'Doherty, 21), but how could paintings such as *D* be termed 'boring'? Just the opposite of boring, one could say. No, Stella's paintings are not 'boring': one could imagine painters such as Titian, Leonardo da Vinci, Diego Velásquez, Rembrandt van Rijn and Rogier van der Weyden being very interested in *D* or *Avicenna* or *Tomlinson Court Park* or *Shama* or *Maha-lat.* Painters, rather than critics, would appreciate and enjoy Stella's irrepressible energy, which has incandescent colours moving in all sorts of directions on slabs of elegantly and intricately curved metal.

Boring art for some is exhilarating art for others, just as erotic art

---

20 see Irving Sandler, *American Art*, 245f, Lucy Lippard, 1966a, 62; Robert Morris: "Notes on Sculpture", op.cit., Kynaston McShine, 1966, Richard Lund: "Why Isn't Minimal Art Boring?", *Journal of Aesthetics and Art Criticism*, vol. 45, no. 2, Winter 1986, 195-7

for some is pornography for others. Thus, James Mellow wrote
that one of Donald Judd's shows was 'one of the most provocative
of the season' (1966, 89). Irving Sandler reckoned that the very
'boringness' of art could be its most interesting aspect. Sandler
said that

> *in its boredom, Stella's painting has affinities to Reinhardt's, but... Stella*
> *appears to have made it the content of his art – a content so novel and*
> *perverse as to be interesting.* (1965, 97)

On 'boringness', Robert Morris wrote that art is found 'boring'
by those who desire 'specialness':

> *Such work which has the feel and look of openness, extendibility, accessi-*
> *bility, publicness, repeatability, equanimity, directness, immediacy, and has*
> *been formed by clear decision rather than groping craft, would seem to have*
> *a few social implications, none of which are negative. Such work would*
> *undoubtedly be boring to those who long for access to an exclusive*
> *specialness, the experience of which reassures their superior perception.*
> (1967, 29)

Minimal artists such as Donald Judd, Robert Mangold, Sol
LeWitt and Robert Morris explored the notions of 'boringness' and
'interestingness'. 'Boring art is interesting art', writes Frances
Colpitt in her book on Minimalism (121). Judd, the chief explicator
of Minimal æsthetics, wrote: 'I can't see how any good work can
be boring or monotonous in the usual sense of those words',
adding: '[a]nd no one has developed an unusual sense of them'
(in K. McShine, 1966). Clearly, the Minimal artists thought they
were making 'interesting' art. Or at least, *they* were interested in
it. If art's good, it can't be 'boring', said Judd, claiming that 'a
work needs only to be interesting'. The discussion of 'interesting',
'boring' and 'value' becomes a quagmire of semantics and the
metaphysics of meaning. Language soon fails to describe the
kinds of intentions that artists have, and the kind of responses that

critics have to works. Robert Mangold said: 'I certainly know whether I'm interested in the work or whether I'm not interested in the work'.[21] Sol LeWitt explained his view thus:

> *I wouldn't say that I wanted to like uninteresting things or to dislike interesting things. I think that's one way that you measure your response, if it interests you. 'Interests' means that it somehow makes a bridge between you and it, you and the object, you and the art object. If it hits home, it means that it's of interest.* (ibid, 121)

Frank Stella's answer to charges of 'coldness' are bemusement: he doesn't understand it. When critics talk about his life and biography, he is annoyed that they aren't concentrating on his painting:

> *I guess I don't mind saying it: for critics who are not first-rate, there is a tremendous assumption of artistic humility, which I didn't seem to have: too much success and being too smug about it. There is no suffering. There is no feeling. There is no questioning. I just keep doing it, and I don't have troubled periods, I don't have crises and anxieties and all that that are documented on the canvas. Basically what they're after is that it's too easy for me, so, therefore, it couldn't be any good.* (E. de Antonio, 114)

Frank Stella seems to be one of those artists lucky enough to be permanently inspired. He is not angst-ridden and obsessed. He is the opposite of passion-driven artists such as Michelangelo Buonaroti and Vincent van Gogh.

One might see Robert Ryman's white-on-white paintings as unsensual, flat, 'boring'. In fact, Ryman's paintings are very powerful. The surfaces themselves are highly poetic, but Ryman also moves towards the state of sculpture, like Frank Stella, with his use of many different materials, from wood to steel, from fibreglass to Plexiglass, from cardboard to copper.

It would be hard to see Sol LeWitt's cuboid, mathematical, conceptual sculpture as sensual. LeWitt's angular objects – the

---

21 Quoted in F. Colpitt, 121.

frames of cubes painted white – seem to be the antithesis of sensual art.[22] His art is all about ideas: the initial idea, the conception, is everything. As LeWitt said: 'all of the planning and decisions are made beforehand and the execution is a perfunctory affair. The idea becomes a machine that makes the art.'[23]

Much of contemporary sculpture consists of hard-edged cubes or rectangular slabs. Whether this use of such stark mathematical forms as cubes is rational or intuitive, it takes a scientific, numerical approach to art to extremes. The idea, Donald Judd wrote, is to simply do 'the next thing': 'one thing after another'. It is a strategy that is not called a strategy, a systemless system. Of Stella's paintings, Judd wrote that the 'order is not rationalistic and underlying, but is simply order, like that of continuity, one thing after another' (1965, 82). The notions of Minimalism – seriality, succession, progression, repetition, permutation – have been around for a long time. Leonardo da Vinci, one might say, painted the same picture in different ways, often abandoning projects before completion.

But, whether the 'system' is serial or modular, whether there is progression or simply repetition, the notion of Judd's, 'doing the next thing', 'one thing after another', explains so much of Minimal art. It explains so much of Judd's work, for instance, those 'ladders' of forms ascending to the ceiling in bronze or plastic, and those long lines of curved shapes set on a wall. It also describes how artists simply go on making work, as variations, or repetitions, or progressions, like Mark Frank Rothko with his many canvases that explore different combinations of purple or yellow clouds floating on oceans of red or blue, or Ad Reinhardt's seemingly repetitious but actually methodical explorations of five

---

22 See Ann Sargent Wooster, 1980, 143-7
23 Sol LeWitt: "Paragraphs on Conceptual Art", *Art Language*, May 1969. See *Sol LeWitt*, Gemeentemuseum, The Hague 1970, Lucy Lippard: "Sol LeWitt: Non-Visual Structures", *Artforum*, April 1967, Roberta Smith: "Sol LeWitt", *Artforum*, Jan 1975, Ann Sargent Wooster, 1980

foot square black canvases. Minimal ethics can produce some extremes of mathematics and seriality.

•

In the film *Painters Painting*, Frank Stella describes his way of working on the *Protractor* and *Saskatchewan* series:

the edges are actually fairly hard. I mean, they're not soft at all. There's not much bleed in a combination of water-soluble fluorescent and Lenny Bocour Aquatint. You probably can't see the pencil line, but it's drawn out over the canvas first and taped over the line. The tape is pulled afterwards. The color here is... well, it's intuitive or arbitrary or a combination of both. (E. de Antonio, 146)

It is interesting to compare Frank Stella's painterly technique with his contemporary, Kenneth Noland, who said:

Sometimes I apply the paint with brushes, sometimes with rollers... any way that I can get it on where the tactile result is compatible with the nature of the color I'm going to use there... When the color is first laid down, it doesn't have anything to do with the resulting size or shape really. Once you lay it down, you can choose by sight how to bring the total color into a certain quantity... For instance, I could make that picture more square, and if I made it more square, then it would become denser and the color would have movement in it. If I extended it longer, you would have a faster kind of movement. You have a way of getting the color to take on a different degree of speed, translucence, transparency, opacity, density, even to the warmth or coolness for that matter. (E. de Antonio, 84)

Frank Stella's paintings in the 1960s moved from the monochrome of the metallic aluminium and copper paintings to the luminosity of the multiple colours in the *Protractor* series. His work has been through many stylistic changes, as Suzi Gablik writes:

Stella's career... is riddled with stylistic discontinuities. The chromatic patterns of Stella's Protractor series, with their complex Islamic architectural decoration, deliberately brought illusionistic devices back in play, and his recent, very rambunctious, relief-collages have long since left Minimalist austerities behind. ("Minimalism", in N. Stangos, 253)

But his major motif remained constant; the band or stripe, which gives a uniformity to his paintings. On Frank Stella's stripe, Kenneth Noland commented:

It's as if Frank works from the outside of the picture in. I'd always felt myself like I was working from the inside of the picture out, and that the shape was a resulting factor rather than a determining factor. (quoted in F. Colpitt, 54)

Carl Andre remarked on Frank Stella's stripe thus:

Frank Stella has found it necessary to paint stripes. There is nothing else in his painting. Symbols are counters passed among people. Frank Stella's painting is not symbolic. His stripes are the paths of brush on canvas. These paths lead only into painting. ("Preface", *Sixteen Americans*, 76)

Significantly, Frank Stella used the colour black, what he thought was a 'neutral, non-color' (B. Richardson, 3). Of course, black is one of the most beloved of colours in contemporary art – in Ad Reinhardt's and Robert Rauschenberg's *Black Paintings*, for instance.

In the *Black Stripe Paintings* the space between each stripe is smudged; in the *Dartmouth* and later in the *Protractor* paintings, the bands became more and more clearly defined, so that Frank Stella ended up with a clear width between each area of paint. As with David Hockney and Morris Louis and other painters who worked directly onto canvas, Stella's colours fuse with the support and canvas. The realization that the painting is an object in its own right developed in Stella's æsthetics, until the movement into painting-reliefs and then into sculptural paintings, or painterly sculptures, was quite natural.

Early Frank Stella attested the flatness of painting. His famous statement runs thus:

My painting is based on the fact that only what can be seen there is there. It really is an object... All I want anyone to get out of my paintings, and all I ever get out of them, is the fact that you see the whole idea without any confusion... What you see is what you see.[24]

Frank Stella changed his views on space over his career, but in the early 1960s his view was that the painting became an object, and he wished to do away with a dichotomy between the painting as an object and what the paint on its surface depicted.

Any painting is an object and anyone who gets involved enough in this finally has to face up to the objectness of whatever it is that he is doing. He is making a thing.[25]

Clement Greenberg had noted that any painterly mark alters the state of the canvas: '[t]he first mark made on a canvas destroys the literal and utter flatness', he wrote (1961, 106). Jackson Pollock had moved in this direction with his 'non-figurative' skeins of colour.[26] But when one comes upon Kenneth Noland, Morris Louis and Stella one sees the paint straight on the canvas, with no attempts at the usual forms of traditional Renaissance illusion, other than a simple pattern. When one first confronts a Stella or a Louis, and sees the bare canvas, it stops one up short. Something is different about their paintings. One doesn't at first notice what it is. One looks closer: yes, raw canvas can be seen. This bare canvas is not a sly reference on the painter's part to the manufacture of the painting (though it is that too). They are not showing the canvas to show the viewer how the painting is made, much as a movie camera can pull back from a scene to show the lights, crew, director and people standing around bored and smoking and desperate for the lunch break. No, Noland, Louis and Stella reveal the canvas for different reasons. It is a new 'leanness' as Stella puts it. The paint on their canvases is not

24 F. Stella, radio broadcast, 1964, in G. Battock, 158
25 F. Stella, in B. Glaser, 58f.
26 See M. Fried, 1965, 14-15.

'representational', in the usual sense. It is not paintwork referring to something outside of itself. It is there, it partakes of *thereness* or *dasein*, to use the terms of Zen Buddhism and Existentialism, two important influences on contemporary American art.

One of Frank Stella's ambitions, in his 1960s work, was to have painting present nothing more than itself. To be 'presentational' rather than '*re*presentational'. He didn't want people to react in the usual way:

> *I made something and it was available for people to look at, but it wasn't an invitation for them to explore, and it wasn't an invitation to them to read a record of what I had done exactly. In fact, I think one of the things you could say about my paintings, which I think I probably a good thing, is that it's not immediately apparent how they're done. (E. de Antonio, 142)*

Frank Stella has the viewer confront the paint stuck on the bare canvas. A new sort of painting is created. For Sheldon Nodelman, Stella and Kenneth Noland created a new fusion of paint and canvas, so that 'no contrast' will be 'set up between the image-content and the picture-object' (1967, 75). Finally, a painting will become an object, as Jo Baer writes:

> *The last radical paintings to attend figure-ground problems were Noland's circle paintings of about 1960. Painters discarded ground altogether, and paintings became objects altogether. (1967, 6)*

Frank Stella's stripes or bands are a powerful visual element which firmly anchor his paintings. The relation between the shaped canvas and the stripes makes sure that the painting remains intense. In *Chocorua III* (1966), a bright yellow stripe follows the edge of a complexly shaped canvas, creating a luminous zigzag which partially enclosed an equilateral canvas, which is slotted into the larger canvas. This bold conception is made powerful by Stella's use of the yellow stripe abutting a grey stripe, which encloses the pink centre of the triangle. Stripe and shaped paintings such as *Valpariso Flesh and Green* (1963) are typical of Stella's boldness and simplicity: two triangular stretchers are slotted together: one is orange, the other is green, both triangles are painted in stripes.

In many paintings, the stripes 'radiate out from the center of the canvas towards the edge', writes William Rubin (1970, 65). Paintings such as Frank Stella's *Gur* (1968, private collection) and *Sabra III* (1967, private collection) are powerful, relying on a simple geometry – a circle dissected into coloured segments – coupled with blinding colours: pink, yellow, light white, orange, black, purple, blue. Stella is very dexterous at handling colours, at putting colours beside each other. His colours are so exuberant partly because of his handling of complimentary colours, the way he sets yellow next to black, or green next to orange.

The all-over evenness of his paintwork enhances the power of his paintings. As he wrote: 'I tried for an evenness, a kind of all-overness, where the intensity remained regular over the entire surface'.[27] But Frank Stella did not want people to stand in front of his admiring his dexterous skill in painting. He was not 'showing off' gesturally. He did not want attention drawn to the marks he made, but to the painting as a whole.

Frank Stella changed his mind, though: in the late 'maxmimalist' works there is a huge emphasis on gesture and brushwork. Paint is daubed in all manner of gestures on the huge aluminium and steel reliefs. Glitter is stuck the surfaces, the paintings beg for a sensual response.

Frank Stella's supports in the 1980s became increasingly complex, and huge. The Vs, Zs, Xs, Hs, Ls, Ts, Us and polygons of the Sixties dazzle with their simple geometry. Like the Pyramids in Egypt, they are simple shapes, but given a bombastic, decisive, rigorously methodical treatment. The use of monochrome helped to give the huge paintings a pictorial unity. Some of the metallic works are vast. The *Protractor* paintings

---

27 Quoted in D. Wheeler, 204.

combined circles and rectangles, but it is the colours which one notices first, the complex interlocking arches and circles of colours, reds interweaving and over-lapping with yellow, pink, blue, purple, amber, green, black. Incredible colours, in Stella's *Protractor* series, utterly distinctive, visible from a great distance. Kenneth Noland spoke of the physicality of colour:

> *One thing that people don't generally talk about is the fact that the experience of color is tactile. We talk about the relative coolness and warmness of color, or transparency or opacity, and really all those descriptive terms are tactile descriptions rather than to do with the redness of red.* (in E. de Antonio, 84)

Frank Stella's paintings are full of confidence and assertiveness. They are paintings that know exactly what they are doing. They are full of a drive that one might see as ruthlessness, but is in fact the Minimal ethic of taking an idea to its logical conclusion. Stella loves method, like so many artists. One can follow his thinking as he moves from pattern to pattern, from each configuration of colour, shape, support, scale, stripes and space.

7

Later Work By Frank Stella

Since the 1970s and his series of multi-part paintings, *Polish Village* series, *Indian Birds* series, *Brazilian* series, *Exotic Birds* series and *Circuit Paintings*, Frank Stella has been building his paintings out from the wall. 1970 (the year Mark Rothko and Barnett Newman died) was a key point in Stella's career, as Corinne Robins writes – it included the big MOMA retrospective show:

> *1970 becomes a cutoff point for Stella. It was the year he had a full-scale retrospective exhibition of his work at New York's Museum of Modern Art, with a book-length catalog by the museum's director, William Rubin. After the exhibition, and following the short period when he was hospitalized with a knee injury, Stella ceased using stretcher bars as painting supports and began gluing his canvas directly onto cardboard, and then made paint and collage works on cardboard, wood, and finally honeycombed aluminium.* (1984, 198)

Frank Stella too regards 1970 as a key moment in the history of abstract painting, for here post-painterly abstraction had run its course, had 'turned to ashes' (WS, 1).

> *By 1970 abstract painting had lost its ability to create space. In a series of withdrawals, it began to illustrate the space it had once been able to create. The space in abstract painting, in a certain sense, became more advanced – more abstract, if that is possible. It was no longer available to feeling, either emotional or literal. This fulfilled one of modernism's great dreams: the space in painting became available to eyesight alone, but unfortunately not to eyesight in a pictorial sense, but to eyesight in a literary sense... This development is probably easiest to comprehend in spatial terms: what we are left with is illustrated space which we read; what we have lost is created space which we could feel. Put simply, the pictorial space of abstraction has acquired artificiality at the expense of reality.* (WS, 43)

For Frank Stella, post-1970 abstract painting was full of dull, 'inert' space; flat, shallow acrylic surfaces: 'unbearably thin and shallow' (WS, 42-43). Worse, abstract painting he maintains, 'has always been flawed by spatial conservatism' (WS, 43). This statement seems odd, when so many people seem to have problems even now with abstract painting, as if abstract painting were too 'avant garde', too 'mod', too 'difficult'. No, says, Stella, abstraction is not avant garde, it is conservative. For Stella, abstract art 'has rendered itself space-blind' in order to survive, because to survive art must become literal (WS, 46). Abstract art must not let itself be limited:

> *Abstraction cannot accept limitations graciously; it refuses to tolerate the pictorial boundaries so comforting to semi-abstraction.* (WS, 98)

The critical response to Frank Stella's work since 1970 has been varied: there is a feeling that Stella has somehow betrayed his Minimal origins, by this explosion into multidimensional art. Yet, apart from the black, copper and aluminium works, Stella's paintings have always been colourful. The move into three dimensions is not so much of a change of direction as one might at first think. There were suggestions that Stella had a 'failure of nerve' around this time,[28] but the move into the new works seems now to be totally assured. Stella is one of those artists who always seems to know what to do and how to do it. The doubt, the anxiety, the confusion, the indecisiveness of many another artist simply isn't part of the Stella way of working.

At first, Frank Stella's post-1970 works seemed to be 'constructivist'; they were described as 'reliefs' or 'collages'. Stella layered planes on top of each other, and these works of the early 1970s do not seem such a great change from the *Protractor* series, but, rather, an organic development.

The *Brazilian* paintings were much brighter in colour, and were painted on honeycombed aluminium. The forms were layered in relief-style again, in the *Brazilian* series though the use of aluminium marks another change in Frank Stella's painting. The *Exotic Birds*, though, were, as Corinne Robins, notes, 'the very opposite of the artist's approach' (ib., 198). In the *Exotic Birds*, the forms were no longer flat. They curled outwards from the wall, they broke up the rigidity of one flat plane upon another flat plane. Works such as *Steller's Albatross*, of 1976, introduced French and irregular curves and swirls of paint upon cut-out aluminium shapes. The paintings became much freer and more open, quite different from the rigid æsthetics of the *Protractor* and the copper and black paintings. Though the *Protractor* series was very colourful, the move later into three dimensions, and the use of the French curves sticking out from the wall, made for a much more exuberant art. Critic Jeff Perrone was disappointed, claiming that 'Stella had deliberately set out to infuriate the people who found his aluminium paintings last year some of the best modernist paintings ever' (74). Stella, though, still regarded his paintings as modernist, as he said in *Working Space*.

Gleefully Frank Stella explored the possibilities of space and colour, the relation between paint and metal, between texture and

28 P. Leider, 1970, 96

space, in the *Brazilian* and later works. Paintings such as *Maha-lat*, a maquette for the *Indian Birds* series, and 1979's *Shama*, are writhing masses of curving metal. The edges of each honey-combed aluminium slab are left open, as the shapes of the aluminium show. Sometimes Stella paints these edges.

The multi-media paintings of the post-1975 era required a new dexterity, a new handling of space and light and colour. The artistic problems were so much more complex in these 3-D works, but, as André Gide said of artistic problems, the problems were solved by the work of art itself. The space of the new works is not Cubist, nor Constructivist, as Noel Frackman notes, saying that the

> *staggered sense of angled rectangles subverts the idea of the existence of any single picture plane and, beyond that, the very nature of the space of abstract expressionist painting. In these works there would seem to be at least three picture planes or maybe four, if we include the curved rectangular forms themselves.* (1976, 125)

The paintings of the 1980s became deliriously three-dimensional, though Frank Stella claims they remain 'paintings', not sculptures. Stella's new works are as exuberant and as colourful as art can be. They are so startling in their sheer pleasure and enthusiasm that some people might be put off by them, observing them with suspicion. Works such as *Thruxton 3X* are explosions of light, colour, texture, shape, pattern, volume, space and multi-media extravagance, an æsthetic assault. In *Thruxton 3X* there are some six or seven curved slabs of aluminium floating about above other slabs of metal. Some of the slabs are tilted away from the wall, some are parallel to it. The lower left slab is painted white with black squares and shapes crisscrossing over it; yellow has been dabbed on top of these, with red touched in. A long snake-like shape is placed over the top of the painting, moving behind some layers of metal, and over others. It is painted roughly in dark rose and dark ultramarine. The layers behind the topmost slabs are painted in green and yellows and blues, while the sections near the floor are green and dark blue.

At times, Frank Stella's maximalist paintings draw on decorative schemes such as Islamic arabesques, as in his *Protractor* series, at other times his decorative paintwork resembles Western traditions such as the costumes and sets found in circuses, fairs, jesters, harlequins and pantomimes, or interior decoration in the manner of William Morris and the Pre-Raphaelites, or Henri Matisse in Morocco, or Pierre Bonnard's colours in the late paintings of his wife taking a bath. Works such as *Diavolozoppo* (1984) are constructed out of as many materials as the painter can get his hands on.

The Try Works employs huge slabs of aluminium pressed into elaborate French curves, layered over each other, painted in wild reds, blues and pinks. *La Vecchia dell'orto* employs various suggestions of illusion, including a motif quite common in the post-1975 works, a tube-shape painted in stripes, the stripes being grouped in a certain way to give the impression of three-dimensions. In *La Vecchia dell'orto*, the ubiquitous Stella stripe is used to describe semi-3-D forms, a mass of cones and cylinders which intersect. It's a new sense of space in the Stella spectrum of colour and form. The cones or cylinders are sometimes actual cones or cylinders, made from curved pieces of metal, as in *Corposenza-l'anima* (1987). The colours here – bright lipstick pinks, pastel greens and brilliant yellows, connote nothing less than, well, happiness.

There's no denying that Frank Stella's later work is largely positive thinking and full of satisfaction. These are expressionistic paintings, with their wild colours and mad cavorting shapes, but they are as far from the German Expressionists such as Max Beckmann and Emil Nolde as possible. Not for Stella the weighty, tragic emotions of Expressionism. No, his works are full of dazzle and lightness. *Guadalupe Island, Caracara*, a huge honeycombed aluminium painting in London's Tate Modern, is dappled with orange, pale blue, red and pink. The colours come out of heavyweight Expressionist painters such as Emil Nolde in his landscape watercolours, or Ernst Kirchner at his most lurid, but Stella's incandescent colours do not connote, as with Mark Rothko or Barnett Newman, a sense of tragedy and passion. Such an emotive subtext is anathema to Stella, although he talks about painting in Romantic, subjective and expressive terms in his book of lectures, *Working Space*.

In paintings such as *Guadalupe Island, Caracara* and *Shards III* (1983), the paint is applied thickly, with a large brush. There is no attempt to smooth over the edges, or to provide an even surface to the paint, as with the Sixties *Protractor* paintings. Rather, Frank Stella draws attention to the expressive qualities of his brushwork, as with William de Kooning or Julian Schnabel. The expressiveness of Stella's gestures becomes an important element in the painting. The brushstrokes are not hidden as in Barnett Newman's art, who painted with a small brush in small strokes, building up his layers of paint carefully, so that no brushstrokes showed. Stella, rather, constantly draws attention to his brushstrokes, to the very manufacture of his paintings. Works such as *La Vecchia dell'orto, Guadalupe Island, Shards II, Steller's Albatross* and *Shama*, open out to reveal their manufacture. In the 1960s, Stella used bright colours, like Morris Louis, but kept them neatly bounded within their stripe patterns. The late maximalist works continually refer to the making of paintings. For Stella, the artist is a privileged participant in the making of art: the 'audience' or viewer is always one step away, is always 'after the fact': '[t]he sensation is one that the artist experiences as the first and only necessary viewer' (WS, 127).

The Stella exhibitions of the late 1980s and early 1990s were colourful affairs, in which one was impressed by a sense of colour and light, a spaciousness to the works, and a huge scale, so that each work dominated the gallery rooms. Stella is in no way a quiet, unobtrusive artist: his paintings are domineering, self-confident, assured of their own effects. Stella has always been an artist who knows what he's doing. His paintings do not lurk in gallery corners, shyly. His paintings announce themselves instantly and powerfully. Stella's paintings says *look at me*, and one has to look. Stella's June-July, 1985 show at the Institute of Contemporary Art in London was typical: massive multi-media works were squeezed into the ubiquitous sparse white rooms, completely taking over the staid spaces.

In *The Waves: 1985-1989*, a show at Waddington's Gallery in London in November, 1989, Frank Stella showed a number of screenprints with lithographic and linoleum block printings, hand-colouring, marbling and collage. The multi-layered prints involve a host of printmaking skills, from marbling to screen-printing. The result is a rich multi-media feel, where images stolen from photography mix with the hand-crafted touch of lino cuts.

In *The Waves*, Frank Stella's prints are as colourful as ever: luminous, fluorescent green and pinks and yellows are sedated by greys and blacks, though there is much white space. Using paper and card and staples enabled Stella to create complex layers of illusionism and abstraction quickly. The paper also enabled Stella to move the pieces around before stapling them down – it's not so easy to move heavy bits of metal about in the same way. *The Waves* series of thirteen screenprints veer between figuration and abstraction. Though mostly abstract, there are recognisable patterns – and quotes, as with Jasper Johns, from earlier works.

In *Moby Dick*, for example, made in a print edition of sixty, there are stripes in concentric curves, recalling Frank Stella's *Protractor* series. In amongst the rich patterns, *Moby Dick*, as the title suggests, offers remnants of representation, a rounded whale shape in grey and black moves across the centre of the print. This may or may not refer to the famous whale in Melville's great American novel. *Going Abroad*, also from *The Waves* series, put together hand-coloured collage, marbling, lithography, lino cutting and silkscreen printing into one place, a large framed picture, 73.4 by 54.7 inches. These large prints are impressive, and self-consciously refer to their facture, as Stella glues and staples together many different kinds of paper and card and media.

Large-scale projects of later years have included the lobby and interior of Toronto's Princess of Wales Theater (1993); the lobby and theatre of the Moores Opera House in Houston, TX (1997), dubbed the 'Stella Project'; a sculpture in Washington, DC; and a bandshell in Miami (2001).

In 1994, Frank Stella showed a large number of works in London's premier commercial gallery district, Cork Street. The notion of 'paintings' as sculptures was dropped, and the three dimensional works were called sculptures by the artist. Stella's 1994 sculptures were abstract works, made with stainless steel welded into impossibly entangled configurations. What is most obvious about some of Stella's late sculptures is the lack of colour: many of the sculptures are lacking altogether in paint and colour. Gone is the lush multicolour, to be replaced by the cool grey of stainless steel. The sculptures at Waddington's, London, were set in the middle of the gallery, while the more recognisably Stellan paintings were ranged around the walls.

In the 1980s, Frank Stella started to merge the heavy 3-D style of the paintings with the flat, layered quality of his prints. The July 1994 show at Waddington's Gallery, London, called *Imaginary Places*, featured many large paintings, some of them 9.6 feet wide, made from pieces of paper and card stapled on top of other pieces of paper and card. Instead of using metal, Stella made the paper and card do the work of creating the 'working space' around a painting, which is so important for him. The layering of paper makes for a quite different effect from the metal chunks being built out from the wall.

Paint has been laid on thickly for a long time – think of J.M.W. Turner's late oils, or Vincent van Gogh in canvases such as the famous *Wheatfield with Crows* or *The Starry Night*. Certainly van Gogh's painterly surfaces, like those of, say, Henri Matisse or Pierre Bonnard, are very erotic, with their feverish brushmarks laid on top of each other. Perhaps the eroticism of van Gogh's paintings plays a part in the fact that his works command higher prices than any other artist: $53.9 million for *Irises*, and 82.5 million dollars for *Portrait of Dr. Gachet*.[29]

But Frank Frank Stella's massive mixed media structures are truly wild, like orgasms of paint, metal, fibreglass, ink and crayon. Stella has very decisively and joyfully exploded the traditional easel kind of painting, where everything sits neatly within a box-like frame, on a flat, illusionistic surface. Painting has to be trapped in a 'perspectival box, a container for measurable space... a free-floating cube', and unless it is inside the box, says Stella, 'we tend not to like it' (WS, 64). Stella's new works systematically demolish the traditional, academic notion of painting as a rectangle of illusion. For there is no illusion in Stella's works: they are not depicting anything other than themselves, with their squiggles and zigzag patterns, their fluorescent pinks and lurid greens, their splotches and dabs and overpainting. For Stella, abstraction today has become average and 'illustrational', it is not radical, but ordinary (WS, 65-66). For Stella, abstraction needs to be a million times more daring: 'abstraction has to recognize that the coziness it has created with its space of reduced, shallow illusionism is not going anywhere' (WS, 66).

---

29 see Suzanne Munich: "N.Y. Art Auction Scene: A Still Life", *Los Angeles Times*, 17 November 1990, F1, 11

In later works, Frank Stella disliked the flatness of modern painting, and of abstraction in particular: the smooth flatness of Barnett Newman or Jules Olitski or Morris Louis. Much as he admired other abstract painters, Stella aimed to move beyond them by destroying the solemnity of the flatness of modern painting. He writes in *Working Space*:

> *The result of modern painting's restrictive view of flatness has been a negative reaction to the yielding surface of painting. Painting today is trying to be deliberately messy in order to deny the fragility and limits of the surfaces available to art.* (51)

Many modern painters are self-consciously 'messy' – think of John Walker, Michael Porter, Amat, K.H. Hödicke, Enzo Cucchi and Francis Bacon. Freudians have things to say about artists who are deliberately 'messy' – for them it all goes back to anal psychology, toilet training and constipation. Aesthetically, the explosion into chaos and mess helps to renew the connection, as Stella says, with the eroticism of texture, with the sexuality of texture and the sensuality of surface, which has always been a large part of art. Think of Greek sculpture: the smoothness of the marble and stone is crucial to the overall experience of the statue. Similarly with Italian Renaissance painting, with all that punched and embossed gold, which provides the spaceless, divine background to Jesus and the Virgin in so many altarpieces and panels.

8

After Frank Stella

There are many other contemporary artists who have developed out of Jasper Johns' and Frank Stella's post-Abstract Expressionist painting: among the more successful are painters such as Christopher Le Brun, Anselm Keifer (such as in his *Wayland's Song*[30]), Thérèse Oulton, Lance Smith, Hughie O'Donoghue, R. B. Kitaj, Jim Dine and Richard Diebenkorn. Painters who seem to have a direct Stellan component include Brice Marden, Sean Scully, Howard Hodgkin and Gerard Richter. The Minimal sculptors – Donald Judd, Robert Morris and Carl Andre – have acknowledged Stella's importance.

Painting still remains central to contemporary fine art or 'high art'. It has a sexuality of surface that artforms such as photography lack. Graphic art and illustration, too, like advertizing, can be seen as too slick and polished. Digital and airbrush art, like

---

30 Anselm Keifer: *Wayland's Song (With Wing)*, 1982, oil, emulsion, straw on photo, on canvas with lead.

Superrealism, can be seen as clinical and artificial. So clean it becomes fake, synthetic, corporate and plastic art, an art which is delusive and unattainable, because it promises a life bereft of complication and mess, and real life is certainly complicated and messy. Contemporary painting, then, counters this false purity in capitalism, advertizing and digital art by loading its canvases with thick paint and impasto marks, and with all manner of materials, from plants to metal to wood to paper. As with Frank Stella's riotously colourful paintings/ reliefs/ objects, much of contemporary painting moves towards the condition of sculpture.

Other artists who have explored the sensuality of surfaces include Robert Ryman, with his really sumptuous white squares. Ryman explores the mysticality of white-on-white, as Kasimir Malevich had done.[31] Paintings of Ryman's such *Untitled,* a small painting by contemporary standards (53.5 inches square), or the very small *Untitled* of 1961 (12 inches square), display a sense of the tactile to rival Jasper Johns. Ryman's art, like Johns', is founded on the sensuality of paint, of surfaces, of the eroticism of texture. One comes back to this again and again in art criticism, this sensualism of surface. As Lynda Nead writes of Kenneth Clark: 'Clark reads brush marks and lines as though they are part of a symbolic language of sensual impulses, telling traces of sexual desire.'[32]

Ad Reinhardt painted black-on-black squares (though Robert Rauschenberg had painted all-black paintings before Reinhardt). Jasper Johns' use of gray, and Reinhardt's and Rauschenberg's of black influenced other monochrome painters, such as Brice

---

31 R. Ryman: *Department*, 1981, oil on aluminium, 60 x 60in, collection: Rhona J. Hoffman, Chicago. See Carlo Huber: *Robert Ryman*, Kunsthalle, Basel; Nancy Grimes. "Robert Ryman's White Magic", *Art News*, Summer 1968, 86-92; Carter Ratcliff. "Robert Ryman Making Distinctions", *Art in America*, June 1986, 92-97
32 Lynda Nead. "Getting down to basics: art, obscenity and the female nude", in Isobel Armstrong, ed, 206

Marden, Stella and Ryman.[33] There are a host of post-painterly abstract artists who make the sensuality of surface primary in their works: Brice Marden, for instance, with his post-Johnsian oil and wax panels; Jean Dubuffet and Antoni Tapiès love to crowd their surfaces with mixtures of materials;[34] Anselm Keifer sticks bits of straw onto his oil paintings.[35] There are any number of contemporary painters for whom touch and surface are crucial: Julian Schnabel, Thérèse Oulton, Gillian Ayres and Jennifer Bartlett. Sean Scully's painterly surfaces recall Johns' oil and wax treatments, as do those of Howard Hodgkin; Scully's formal innovations with a small separate square canvas pushed into a larger set of panels bolted together also recall Johns' multi-part paintings and Stella's shaped canvases.

Another artist with much in common with Frank Stella is the archetypal Minimal painter, Agnes Martin. Her paintings, in which 'nothing seems to happen', to use a Beckettian phrase, are deeply poetic. They are, like Robert Ryman's and Ad Reinhardt's paintings, flat squares in a human-scale (five foot square, for instance). They have poetic titles: *Mountain II* (1966, collection: R. Solomon, New York), *Drift of Summer* (1965) and *Night Sea* (1963, both Saatchi Collection, London).

Agnes Martin's white paintings are not all they seem at first, as with Frank Stella's *Black Stripe Paintings* and Robert Ryman's work. They are in fact covered with a faint but strictly controlled grid, usually made with a pencil. *Night Sea* is, unusually in Martin's *oeuvre*, a light blue, hinting at nature, at skies and seas.

---

33 see B. Richardson, 1976, 3; F. Colpitt, 29

34 Antoni Tapiès: *Great Painting*, 1958, oil and sand on canvas, 6"6' x 8'7", Guggenheim Museum, New York; Jean Dubuffet: *Run Grass, Jump Pebbles*, 1956, oil on canvas (assemblage), 6'8" x 5'1", private collection, Paris

35 A. Keifer: *Margarethe*, 1981, oil and straw on canvas, 9'2" x 12'6", Saatchi Collection, London; *Nurnberg-Festspiel-Weise*, 1981, oil, straw, mixed media on canvas, 9'2" x 12'6", collection; Eli & Edythe L. Broad, Los Angeles

Martin's painterly reductionism seems austere, but in fact poeticizes the world, as with Robert Ryman or Brice Marden.

There are many artists who use multiple panels or 3-D paintings that more than rival Frank Stella's recent 'maximalist' 'paintings': Elizabeth Murray, for instance, produces marvellous shaped panels (such as her *Simple Meaning,* 1982, collection: Jerry & Emily Spiegel, New York and *Fire Cup*, 1982, Paula Cooper Gallery, New York);[36] Sam Gillam creates complexly shaped 'paintings' (such as *Like Today*, 1985, Monique Knowlton Gallery, New York) which, like Stella's constructs, gleefully smash the primacy of the traditional rectangle in painting; Jennifer Bartlett has explored the dynamics of perception and space using multiple panels and rainbow-curved canvases (in, for example, her *Horizon*, 1979);[37] Robert Mangold (in *Four Color Frame Painting no. 1*, collection: Martin Sklar, New York, for example) explores colour and architecture in his multi-panelled paintings which often contain a unifying element of drawing; and Judy Pfaff's multi-media installations are riots of colour and materials which out-distance Stella in scale and madness (for example, her *N.Y.C.-B.Q.E,* 1987, painted steel, plastic laminates, fibreglass and wood, 15 x 35 x 5 feet, Max Protetch Gallery, New York). Where Stella envisages his constructions still as 'painting', as objects that sit on a wall, like an easel painting, without reference to anything else in the room, Pfaff's artworks are environmental installations. Installation art goes far beyond Stella's painting in some ways.

Frank Stella's *Protractor* paintings remain among some of the brightest and most lushly colourful in art. Painters who have used exuberant colours include Vincent van Gogh, Henri Matisse, Mark

36 On Elizabeth Murray, see Paul Gardner. "Elizabeth Murray Shapes Up", *Art News*, Sept 1984, 47-55; Roberta Smith: *Elizabeth Murray*, Dallas Museum of Art 1987
37 *Horizon*, 1979, enamel, silkscreen and baked enamel on steel plates, oil on canvas, 20 plates, 1 canvas, 48 x 250in, collection: Martin Sklar, New York.

Rothko, Leonardo da Vinci, Rogier van der Weyden and Emil Nolde. Colour has been central to contemporary artists such as Barnett Newman, Clyfford Still, Christopher le Brun, Gillian Ayres, Howard Hodgkin, Kenneth Noland, Jules Olitski, Joseph Albers and others. Painters such as Helen Frankenthaler rejoice in the exuberance of pure colour. See, for example, her *Movable Blue* (1973, Citizens Fidelity Bank and Trust Company, Louisville) and *Nature Abhors a Vacuum* (1973, Andre Emmerich Gallery, New York).

Morris Louis was admired by Frank Stella. Louis was a colorfield painter, who advocated the direct contact with the canvas that characterizes Stella's work. Like Stella, Louis applied paint directly onto the canvas. He poured paint onto the canvas in creases and twists and folds, to produce his deeply saturated furls, blotches and curtains of colour, in paintings such as *Alpha-Delta* (1961, Everson Museum of Art, New York), *Saraband* (1959, Guggenheim Museum, New York) and *Aleph* (1960, collection: del Amo, Madrid). *Alpha-Delta* and *Saraband*). In *Working Space* Stella writes of this new painterly/ Post-Painterly/ colorfield/ hard edge abstraction:

> The free-unfettered access to abstraction's early roots had a wonderful and powerful effect: close attention to the early masters coupled with a natural, relaxed attitude toward enlarged pictorial scale and gesture made exciting painting. Jack Youngerman, Ellsworth Kelly, and Sam Francis took off in what seemed like a marvellous, yet familiar, vector. Helen Frankenthaler and Friedel Dzubas were reaching new, relaxed, lyrical heights. Morris Louis, Kenneth Noland, and Jules Olitski undertook an exotic trip in search of firstness, while Donald Judd, Larry (now Lawrence) Poons, and I laid the track to literalism. (160)

Here one senses Frank Stella's pride in being a part of 1960s painterly abstraction. There is a sense of openness and relaxation in Helen Frankenthaler's and Morris Louis' huge cotton duck canvases stained with colours. The new synthetic paints and the new household paints produced brilliant colours. Louis' paintings are overwhelming when viewed up close. In reproductions so much is lost. It's the same with Rothko, Newman, Pollock, Stella and Motherwell: the scale is crucial. Lucy Lippard wrote in Escalataion in Washington" in 1968: 'a sense of scale is also a *sense* proper. Scale is *felt* and cannot be communicated either by photographic reproduction or by description.'[38] Frankenthaler's *Movable Blue* is really huge, a long horizontal-shaped canvas, twenty feet wide, recalling Monet's *Waterlilies*. Louis' *Saraband* is smaller – 8.5 by 12.5 feet, but the curtain-like flood of colours is spectacular, and consuming.

With Frank Stella's *Black-Stripe Paintings*, one is really surprised by their size. In this they take much from Abstraction Expressionism, but the contact between paint and canvas is new. There is no attempt at tonal, sculptural painting in the art of Louis and Stella. The paint touches the canvas in one flood of colour. Stella's paintings are not aiming at illusionistic space. In contrast, though, Stella moved towards the notion of an illusionistic 'working space' in his later painting, those 'maximalist' paintings/ 'reliefs'. Louis, Stella reckons, suggested a new form of pictorial space in painting:

> What is needed is a serious effort at structural inventiveness. What Morris Louis did for a while twenty years ago, following the lead of Barnett Newman, remains more of a promise than a fulfilment. But if his promise were read rightly – if the structural potential of his spatial dynamics were understood and the disjunctive intensity of his color appreciated – his painting could lead to a new beginning... Morris Louis was nearly the last abstract painter to hint at the potential that abstraction might have for creating a full and expansive pictorial space like that of Rubens. (66)

Morris Louis explodes colour, developing it from Wassily Kandinsky and Henri Matisse. He focuses the viewer on his colours: there is simply the colour on the canvas, with no

---

38 L. Lippard, 1968, 42

references to other things. Yet, of course, Louis' furls, like Frank Stella's black stripes, are also æsthetic structures, which speak of pictorial illusion. There is a structure to Stella's *Black Strip Paintings*, as there is to Louis' furls and curtains of colour. Louis' paintings are not simply paint thrown at a canvas.

Similarly, Jackson Pollock's painting are not the result of random splashes, as if someone's set off some grenades in a row of tins of paint. Stella liked to use paint 'as good as it was in the can' (in N. Stangos, 262). Pollock, Louis and Stella work out their paintings carefully. The paintings are imaginative, artistic works, each speaking of the personal touch and gesture of the artist. Although Louis did not use a paintbrush, his gestures are unmistakable. Stella's marks are apparent more in the later works. In the Sixties *Protractor* series, the paint is applied smoothly, as in Brice Marden's monochrome panels. Yet one can see the personal touch in Marden's paintings: he left a gap at the base of his paintings, and allowed drips to form there.

Frank Stella changed his mind about Morris Louis, Kenneth Noland and Helen Frankenthaler, painters with whom he feels are his contemporaries. In 1972, for instance, he said:

> *What I felt at the time – and I don't feel this now – I felt very strongly that Morris Louis, for example, and Ken Noland and particularly Helen Frankenthaler, in their use of the staining technique, there was identification with the facture and weave and all that, but it still seemed to me basically those stains read quite illusionistically.* (E. de Antonio, 139)

Morris Louis' paintings, with their huge splotches of colour, are, as Frank Stella says, loose, open works. Louis' paintings are free of figurative imagery and illusions, even though the stripes, furls and curtains and star shapes are all æsthetic constructs. A.J. Carmean writes: '[f]or Morris Louis the staining technique was such a breakthrough.'[39] Like Frankenthaler's paintings, Louis'

---

39 A. Carmean. "Modernist Art: 1960-1970", *Studio International,* July 1974, 9-15

staining technique allows for an æsthetic freedom which is refreshing after so much tight, close, dry paintwork, as found in, say, the art of Nicolas Poussin and René Magritte. Frank Stella writes:

> *It maybe that what makes Morris Louis's late paintings so appealing is their peculiar Kandinsky-like understanding of Newman. Louis brought a determined looseness to Newman's abstraction that Kandinsky would have applauded.* (125)

It's true, Wassily Kandinsky would have enjoyed Morris Louis' multicoloured explosions, for example, *Point of Tranquillity* (1958, Hirshhorn and Sculpture Garden, Washington DC), where yellows and oranges predominate, anchored by deep blues and a vivacious green. Stella and Louis are the product of a long tradition in art of broken colour: Titian broke up colour in his late works; Joseph William Mallord Turner did too; the Impressionists broke up colour further; Georges Seurat turned it into dots. Stella is optimistic about abstract painting. He reckons it can become better, more innovative, more expansive. Towards the end of *Working Space* he writes:

> *I offer, for what it is worth, what I think painting as our collective endeavour has to do to right itself. It has to understand its successes better, and it has to understand its sources better. With a better understanding of its accomplishments and its past, painting has to build in order to flower again. The authentic, innovative brightness and expansiveness of the sixties can support structures of even greater light and reach.* (WS, 162)

Frank Stella is aware of his own position in the scheme of things, art historically. He has conscientiously attempted to further the causes of painterly abstraction. He has done this diligently, and also enthusiastically. His natural exuberance is very apparent in his paintings. He believes 'that abstraction faces no limits to expansion and extension' (WS, 164). His latest work shows no sign of flagging in the pursuit of openness and expansion, into ever greater and more startling forms of 'working space'.

Illustrations

Illustrations of some influences on Frank Stella, and works cited in his book *Working Space*.

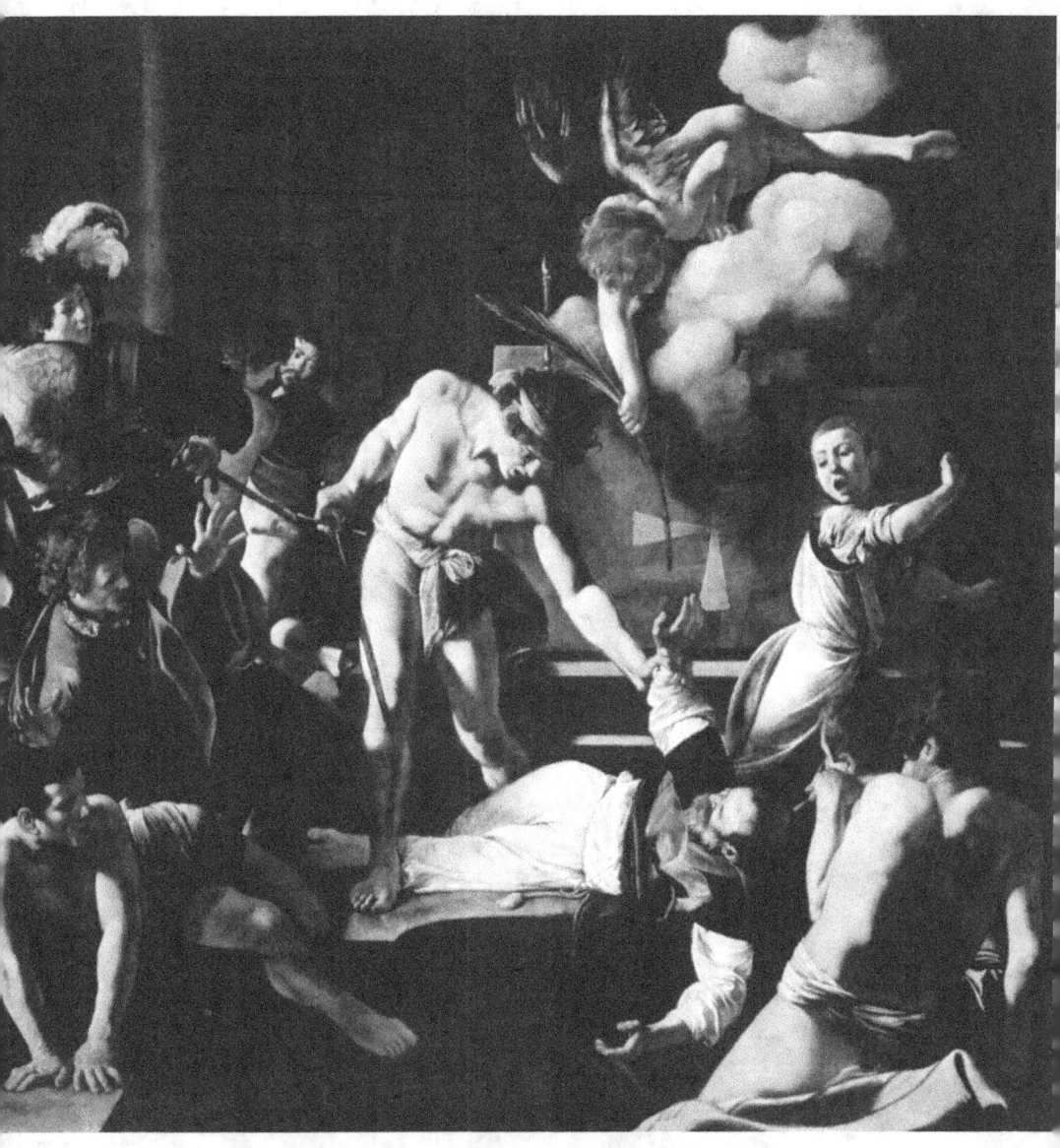

Caravaggio, The Martyrdom of St Matthew, 1600-01,
San Luigi dei Francesci, Rome

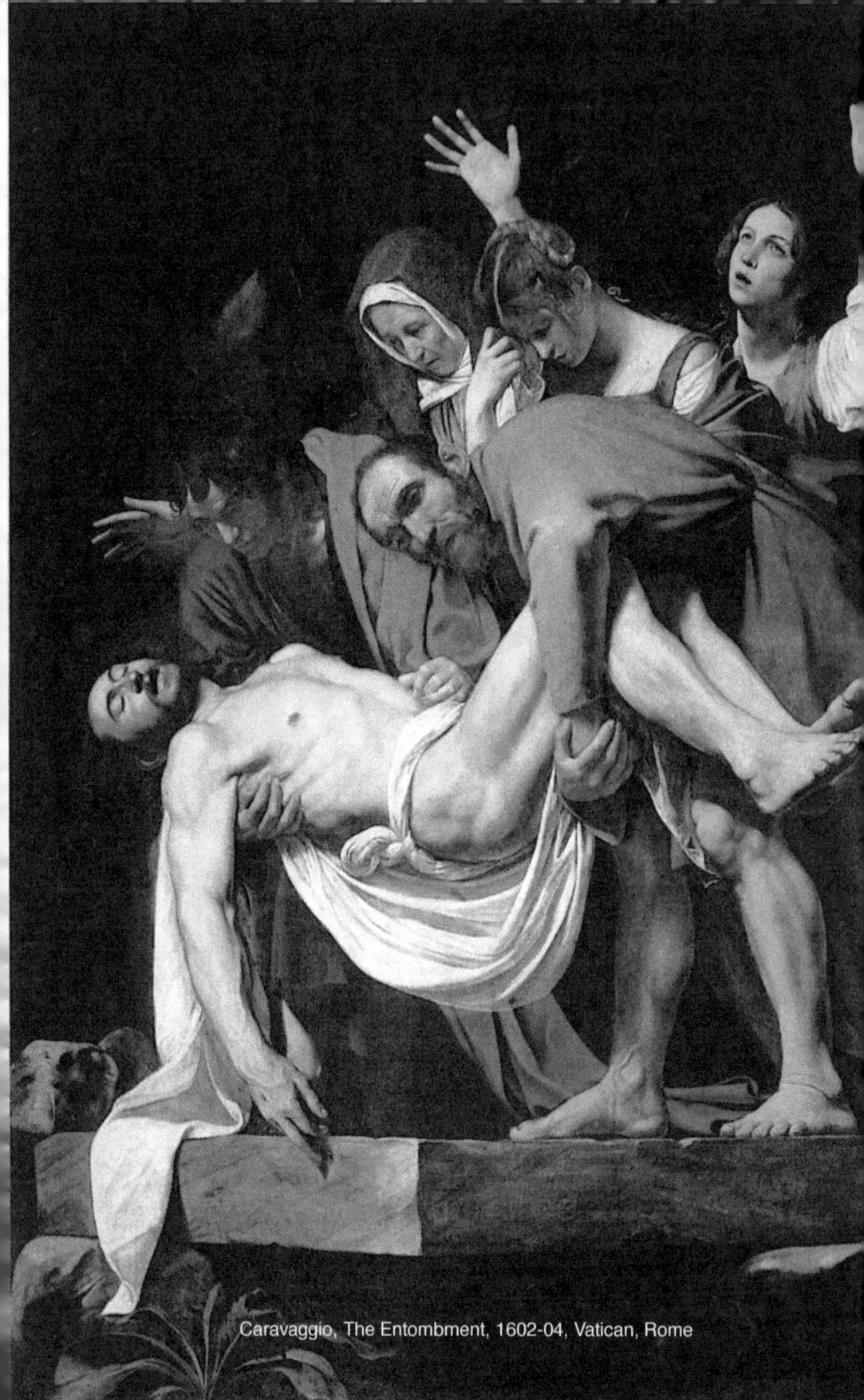

Caravaggio, The Entombment, 1602-04, Vatican, Rome

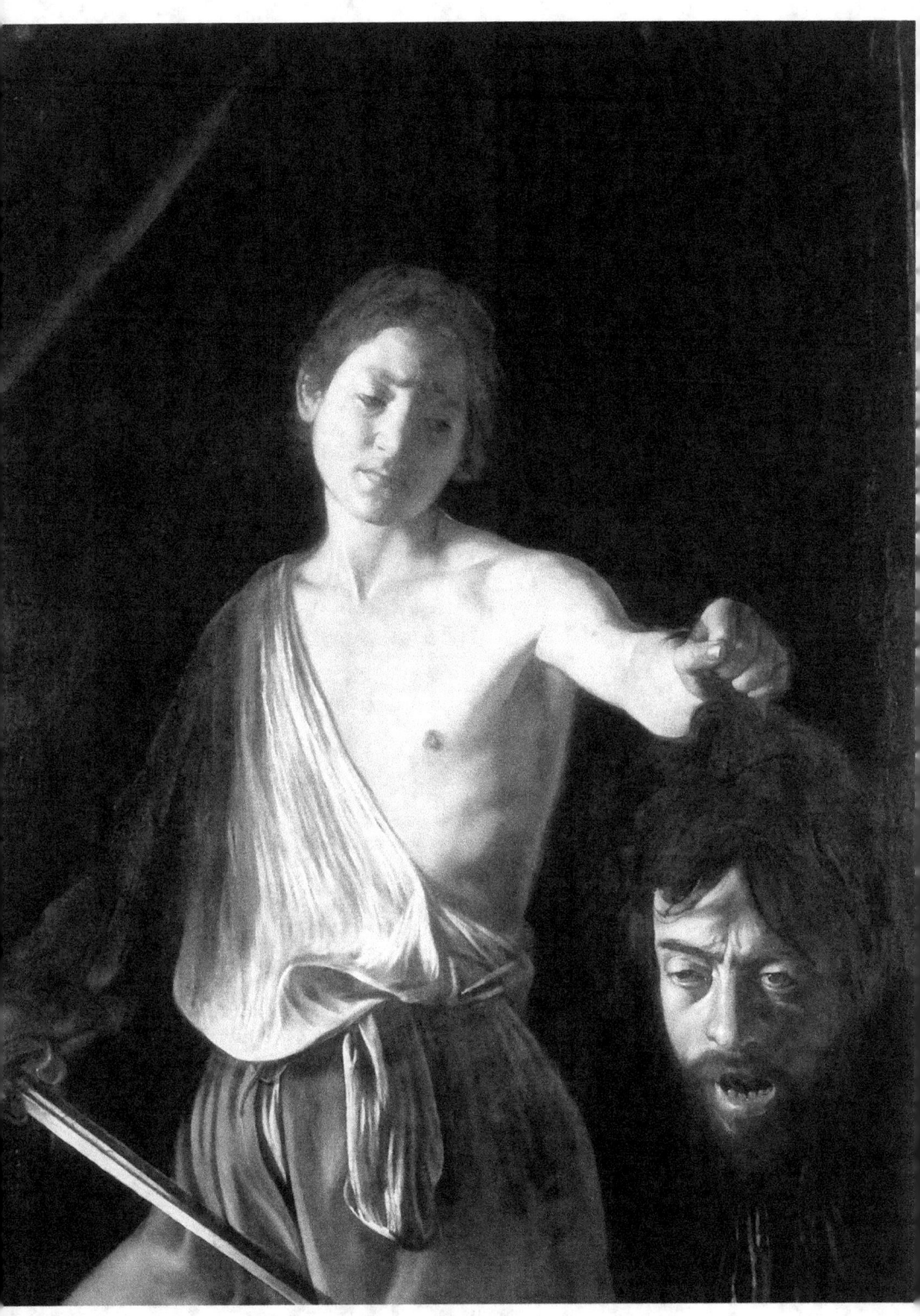

Michelangelo Merisi da Caravaggio, David With the Head of Goliath,
1605-06, Galleria Borghese, Rome

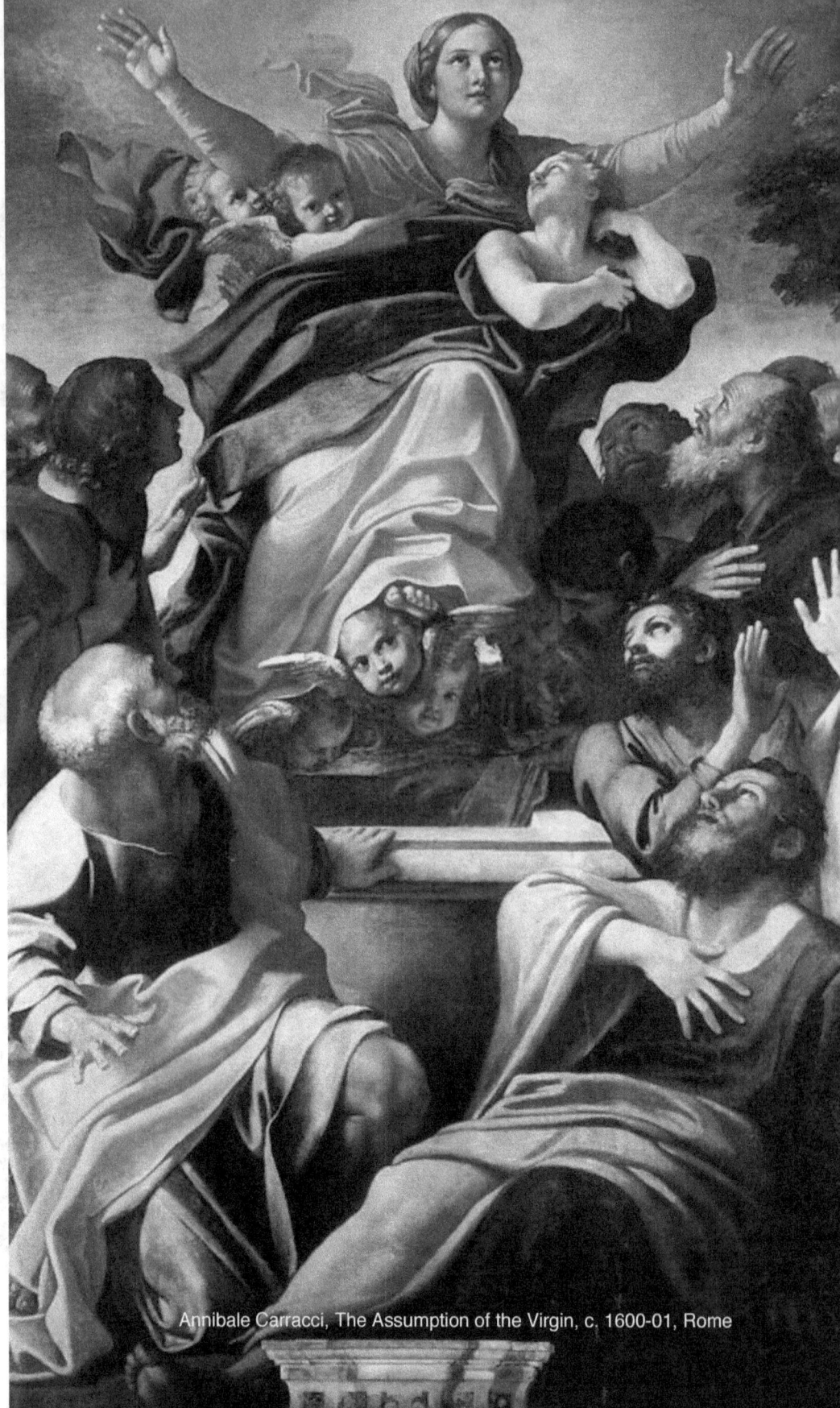

Annibale Carracci, The Assumption of the Virgin, c. 1600-01, Rome

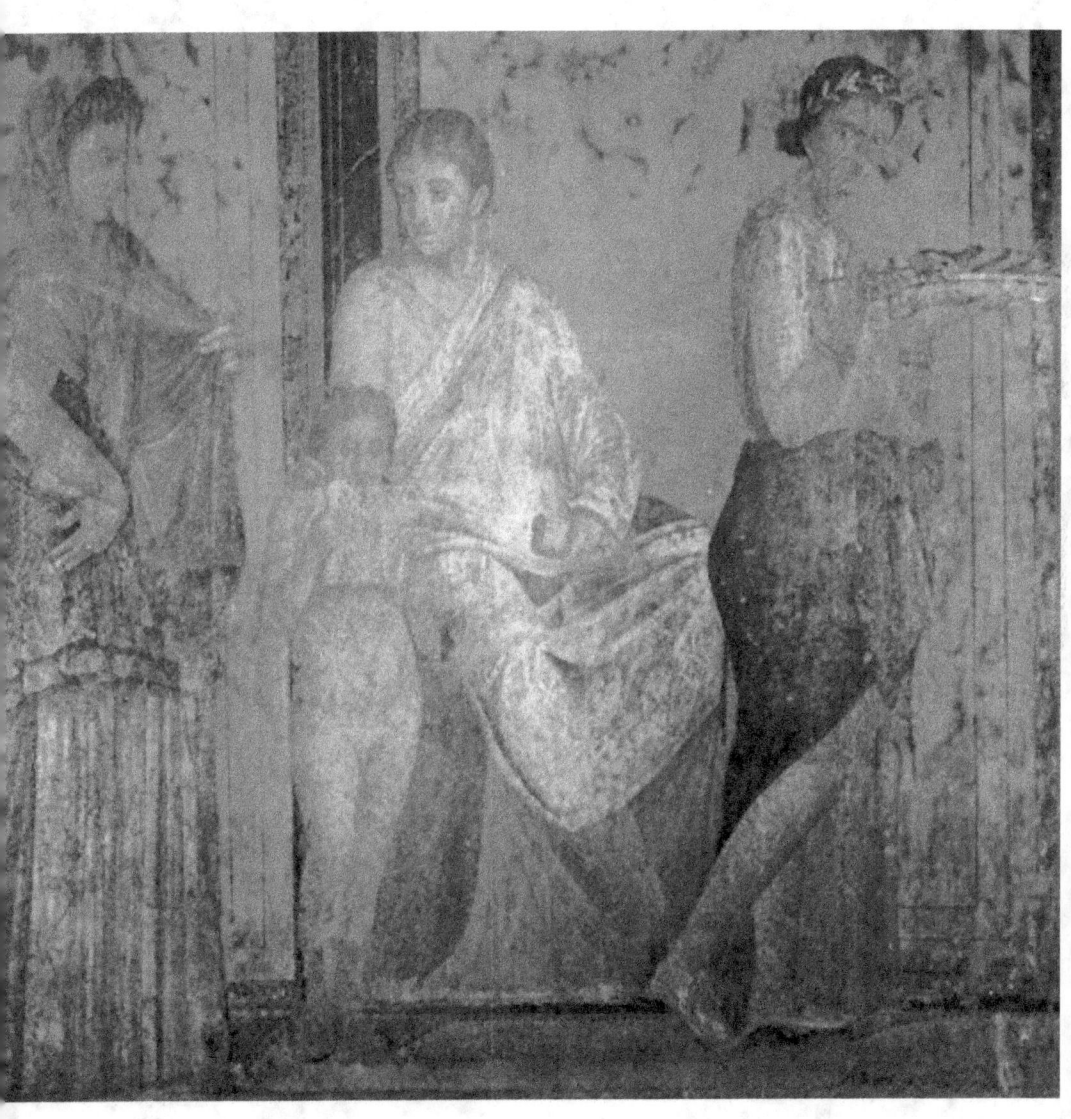

Villa of the Mysteries in Pompeii, c. 50 B.C.

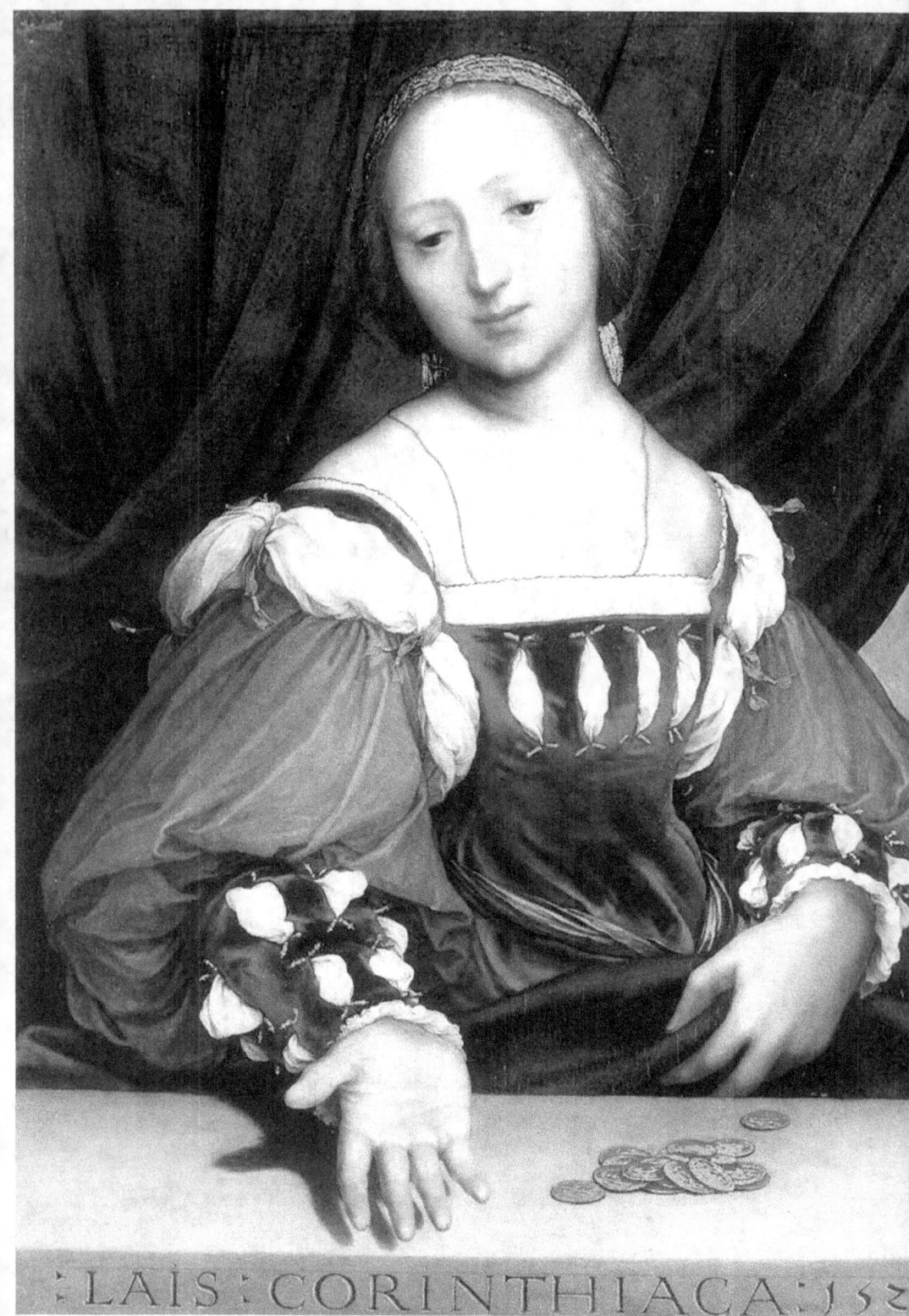

:LAIS : CORINTHIACA : 152

Hans Holbien, Lais Corinthiaca, 1526, Basel

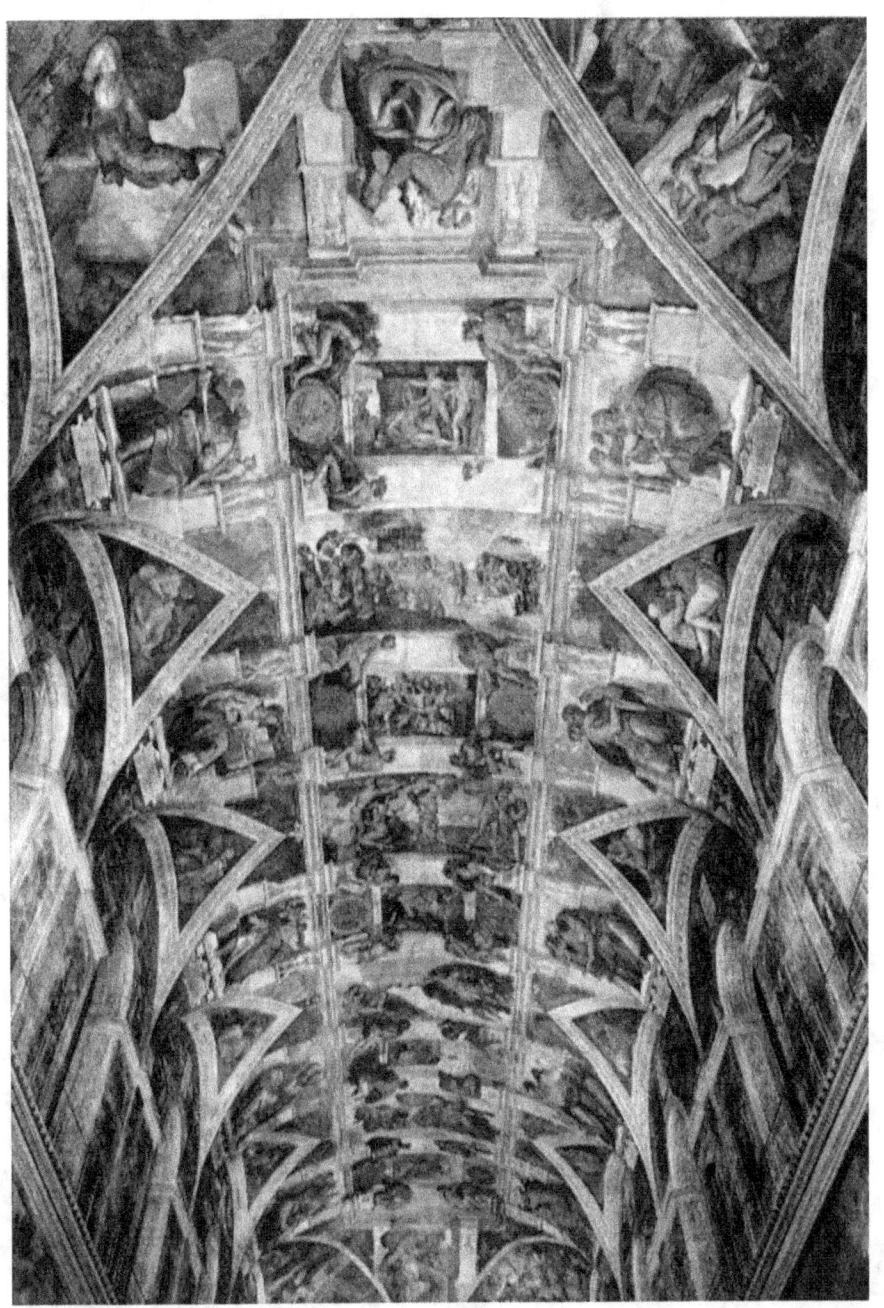

Michelangelo Buonaroti, Sistine Chapel Ceiling, Rome

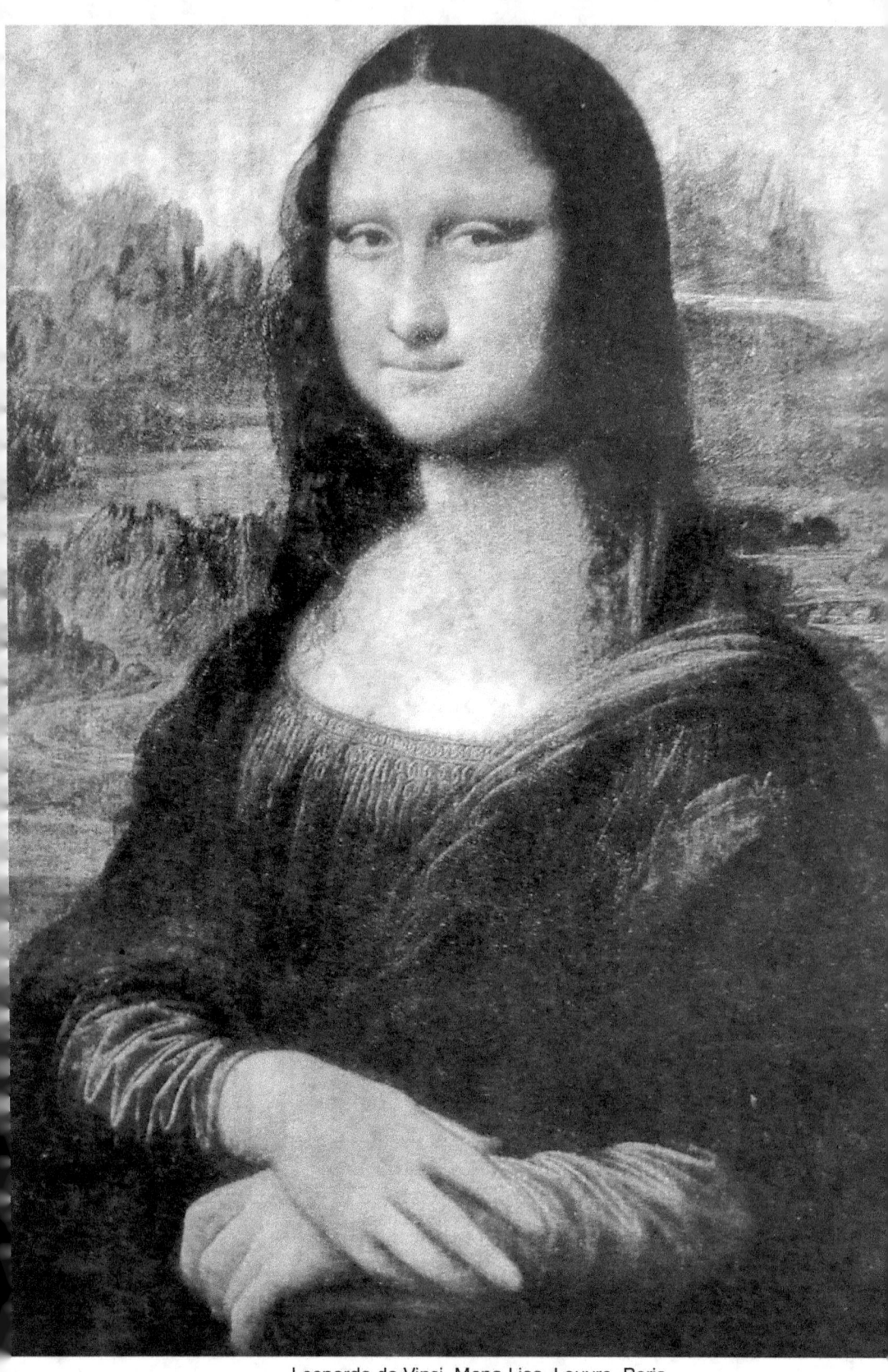

Leonardo da Vinci, Mona Lisa, Louvre, Paris

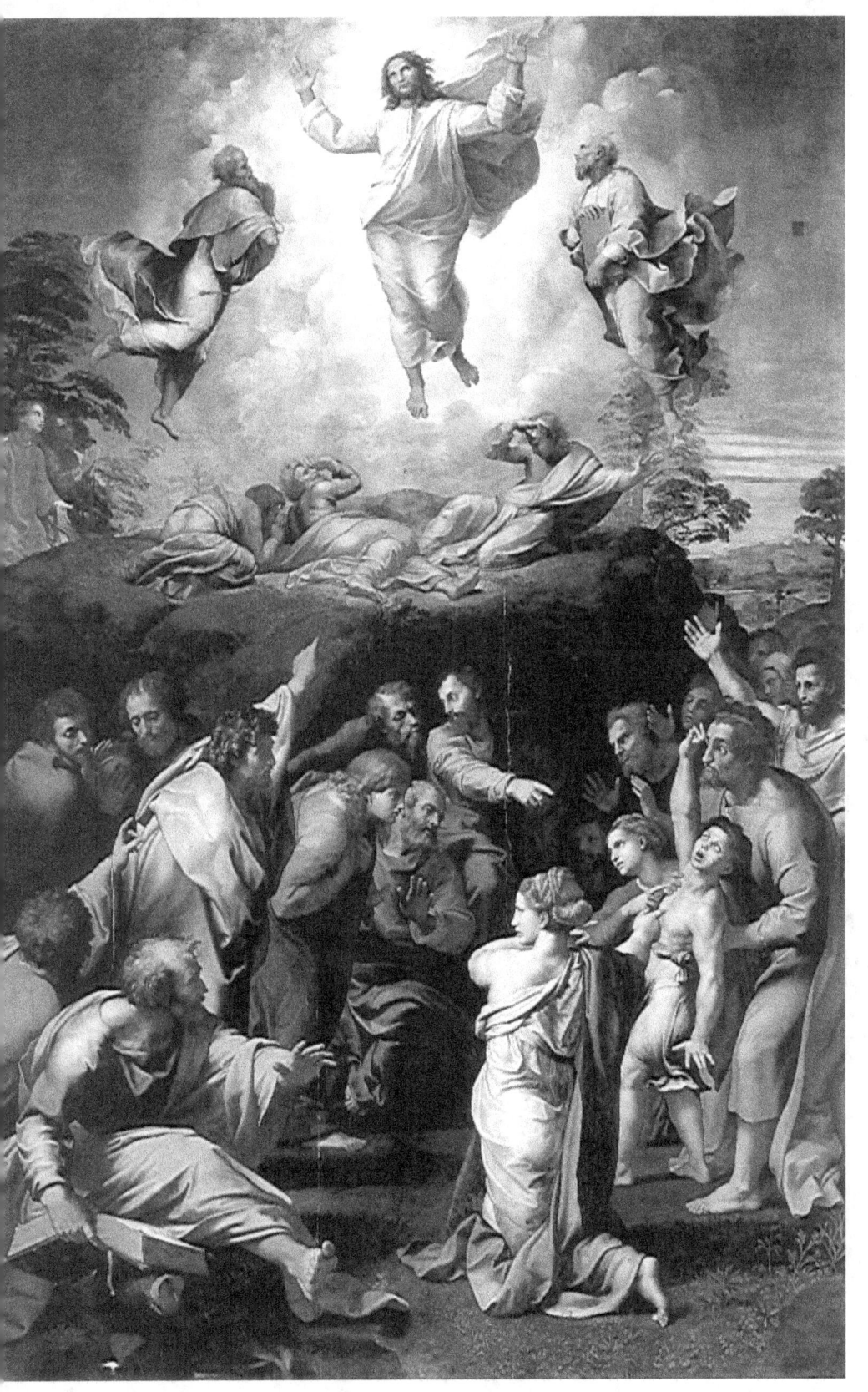

Raphael, Transfiguration, 1516-20, Vatican

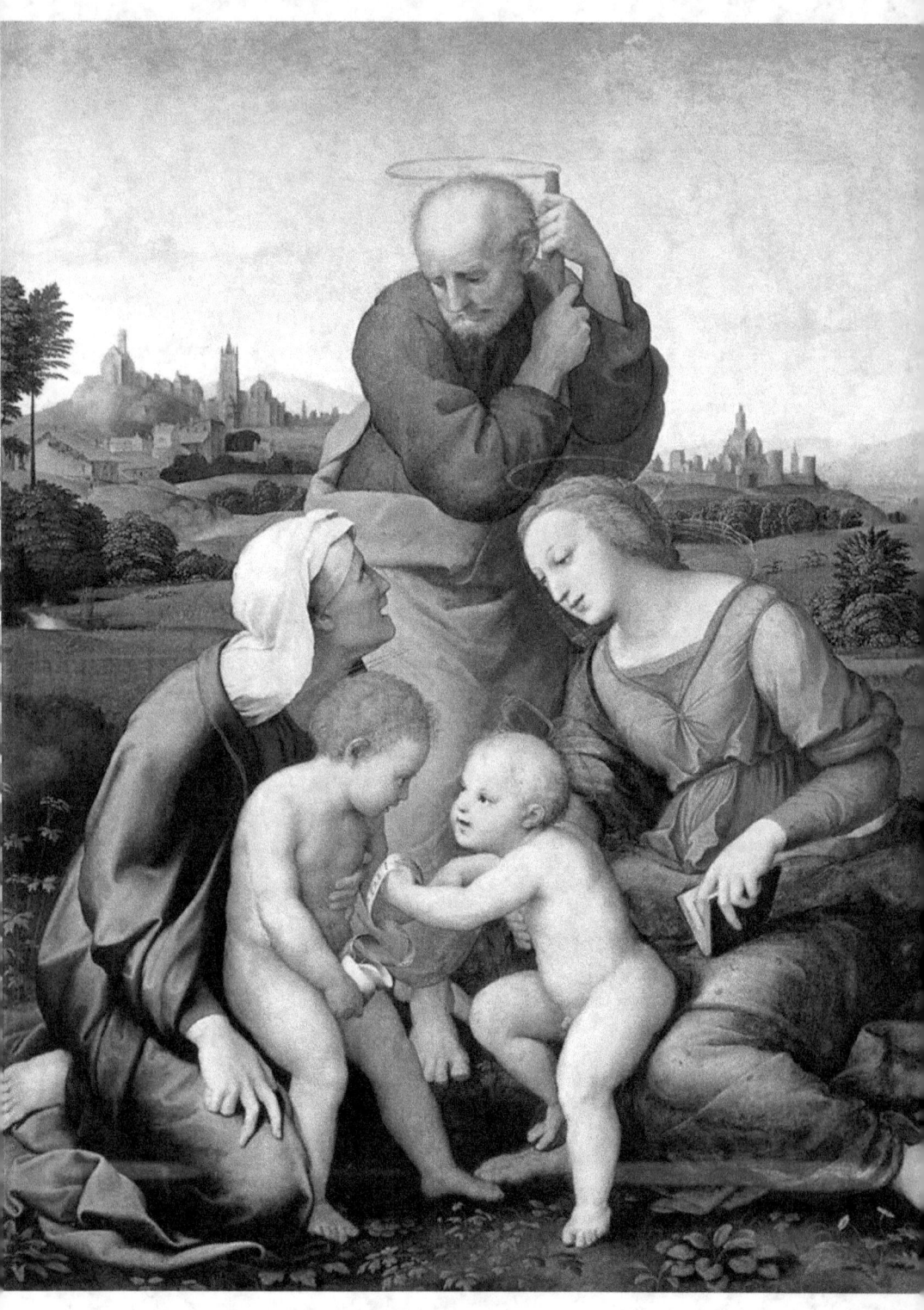

Raphael, The Holy Family, c. 1506, Alte Pinakothek, Munich

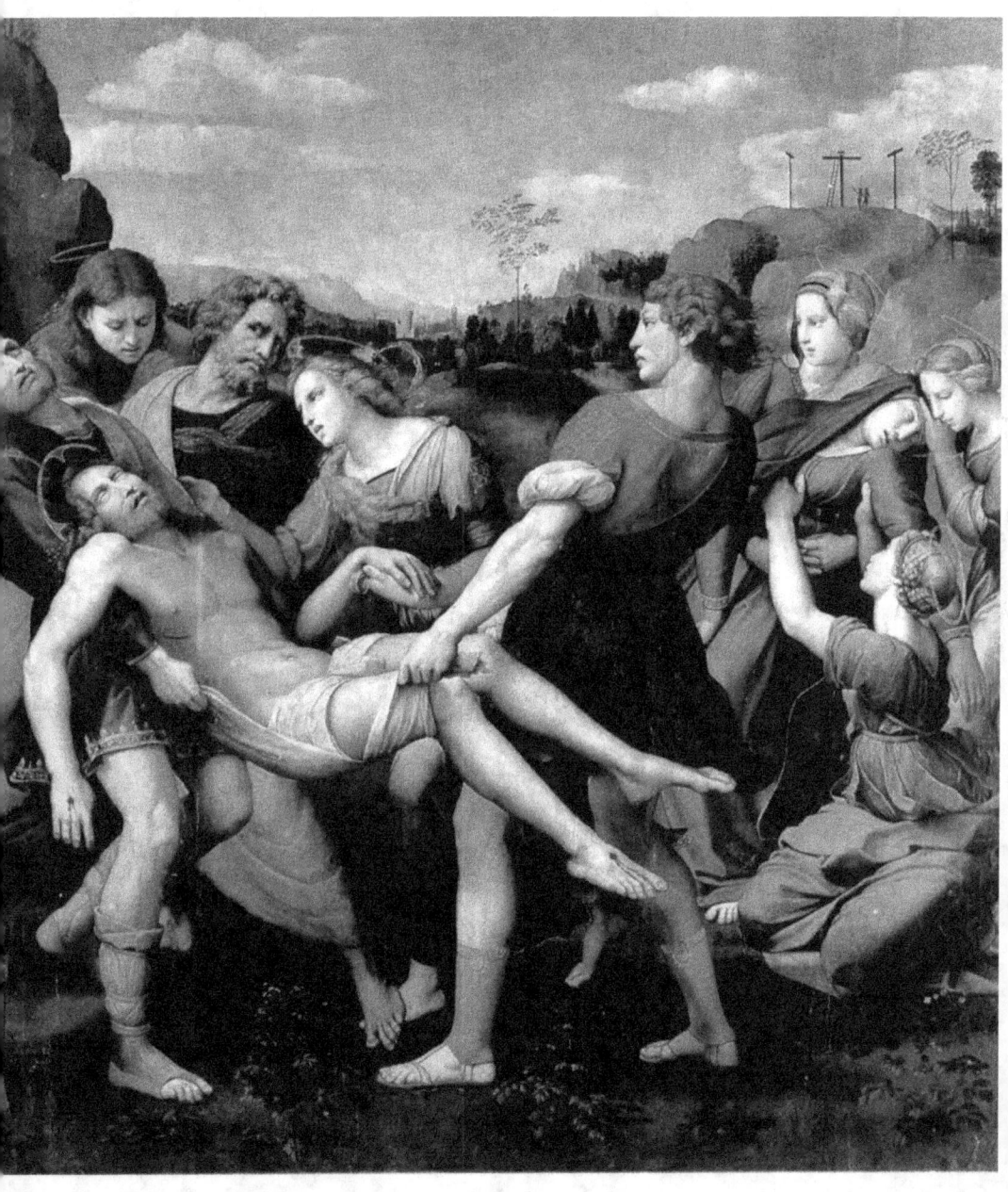

Raphael, The Descent From the Cross, Galleria Borghese, Rome

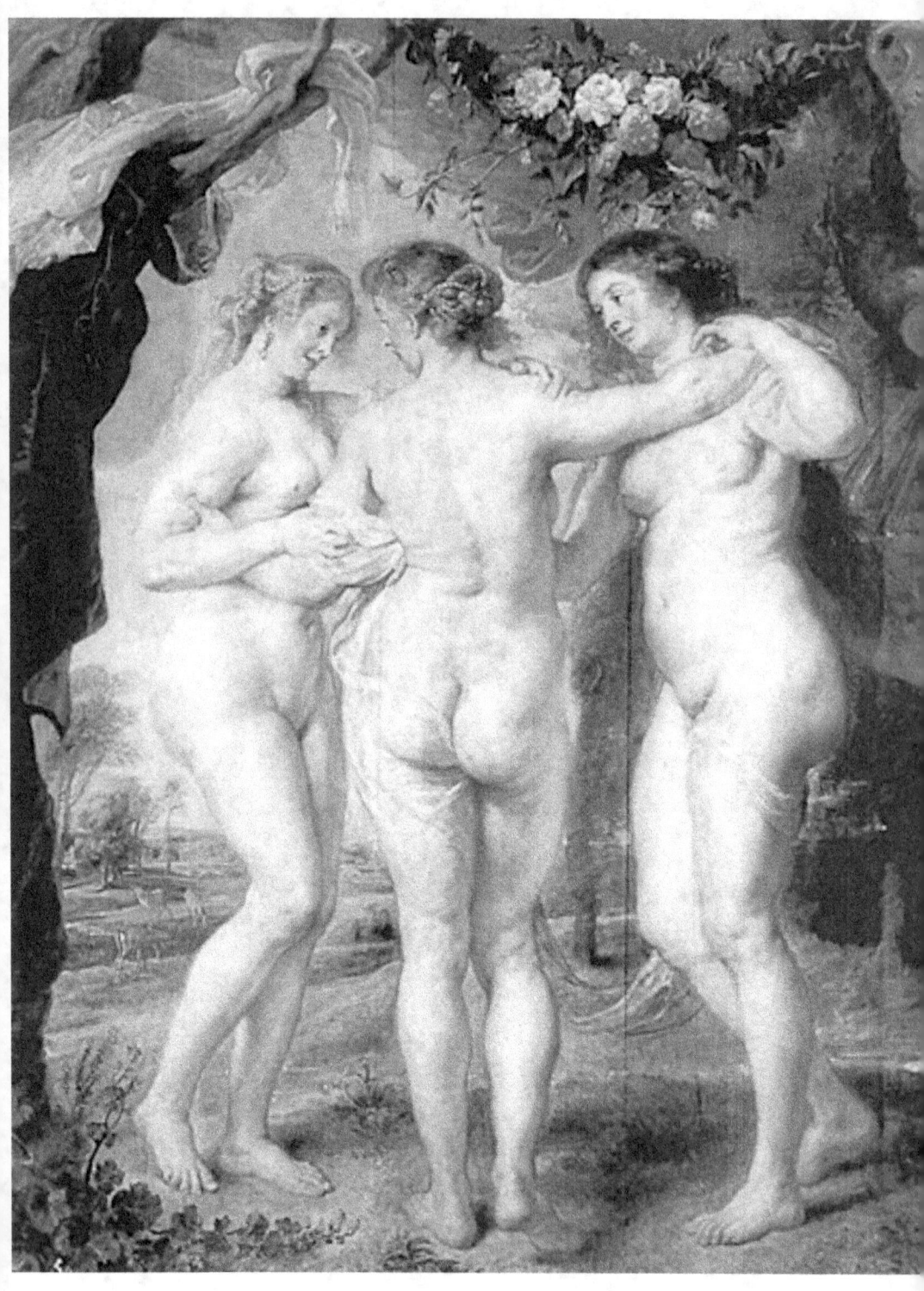

Peter Paul Rubens, The Three Graces, 1638-40, Prado, Madrid

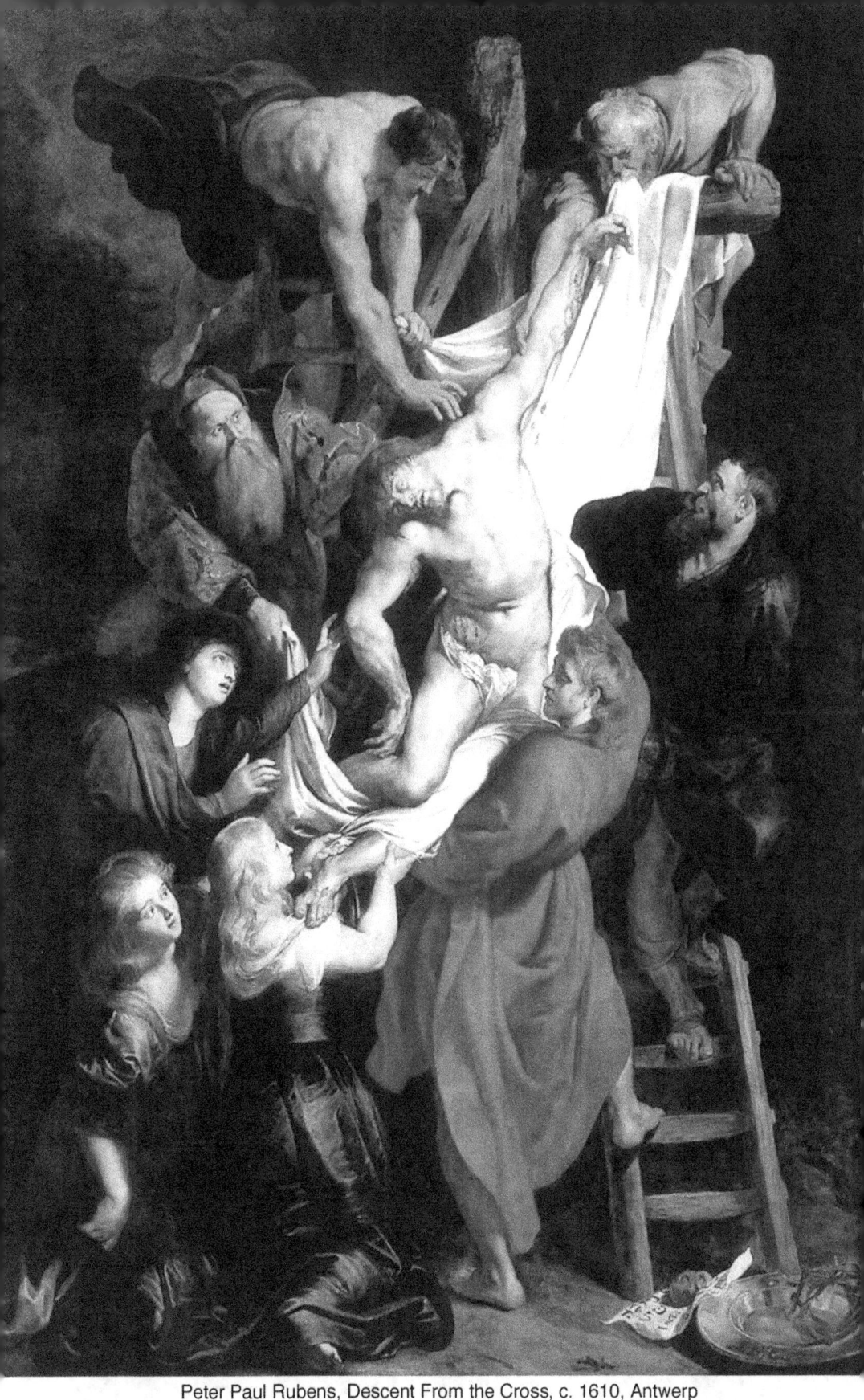

Peter Paul Rubens, Descent From the Cross, c. 1610, Antwerp

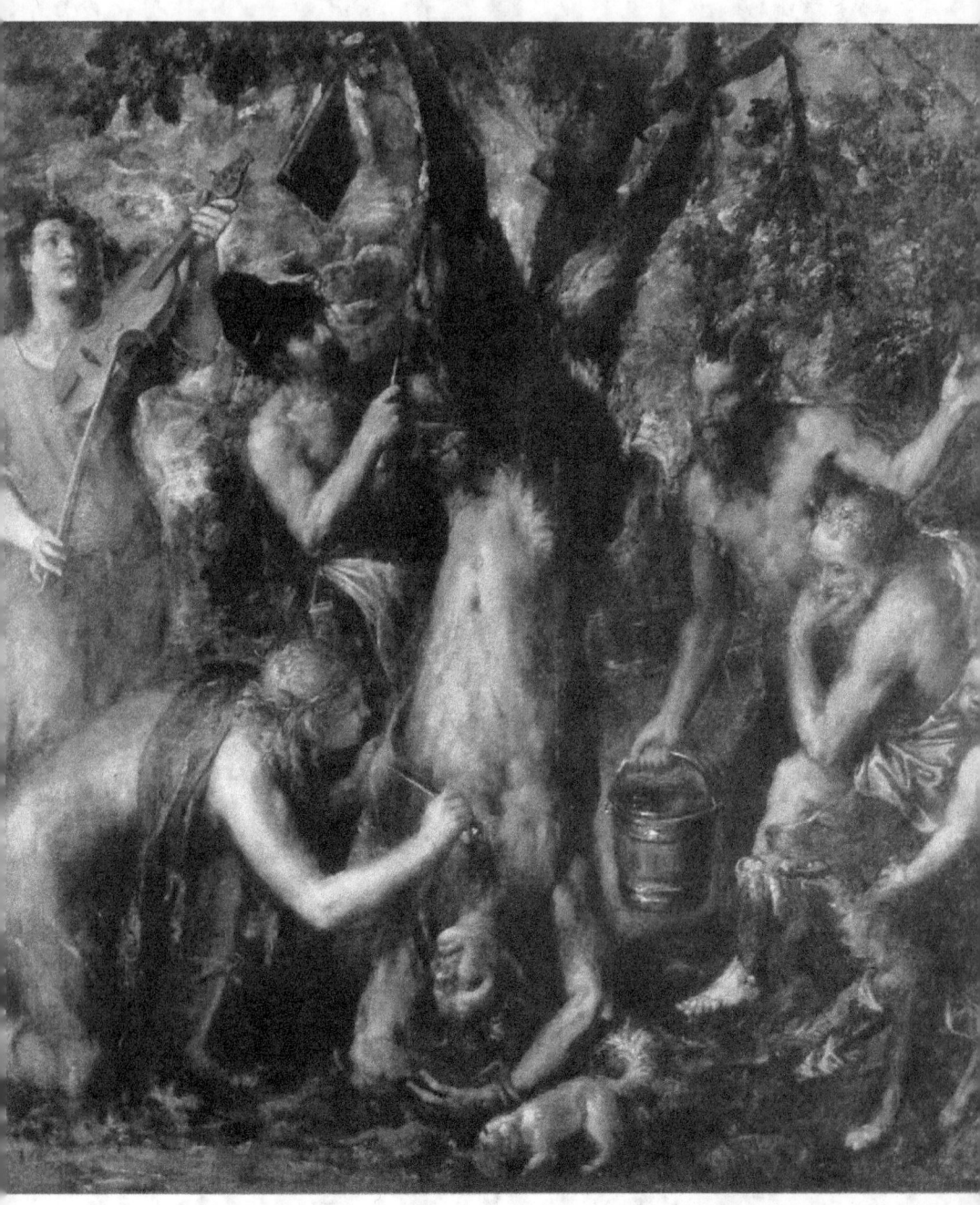

Titian, The Flaying of Marsyas, c. 1570-76, Kromeriz,

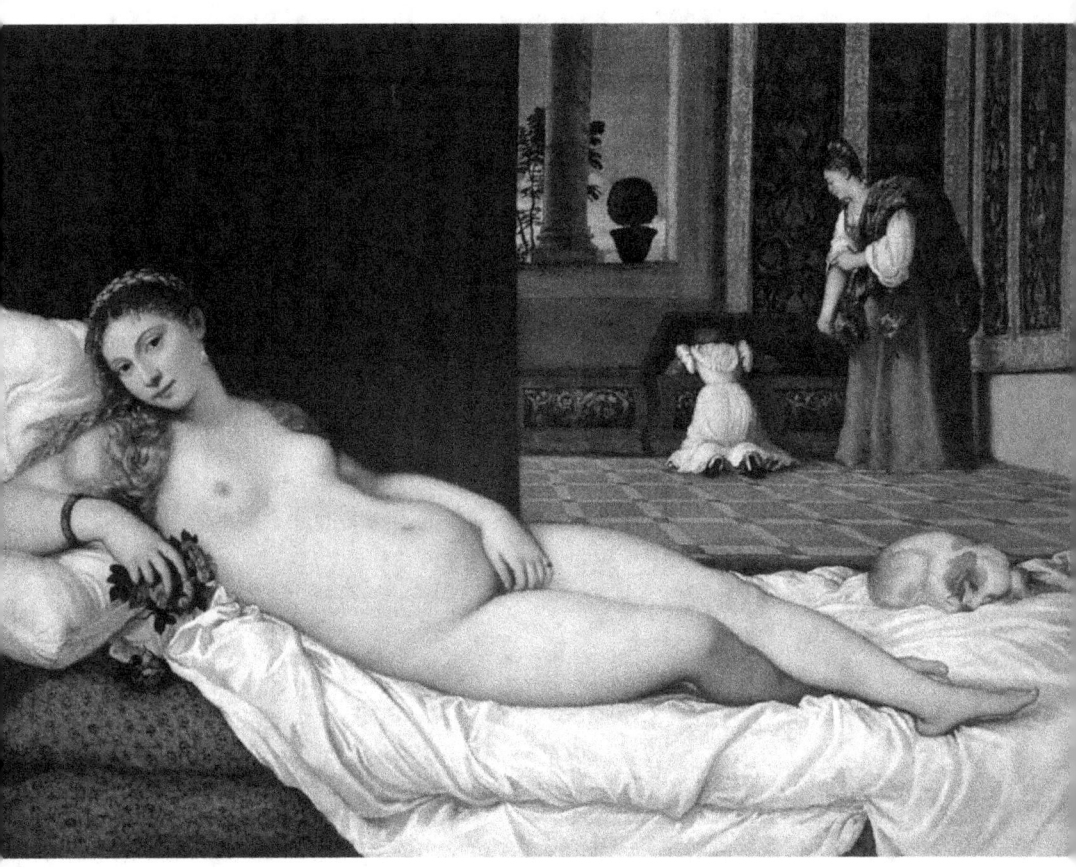

Titian, The Venus of Urbino, 1538, Uffizi, Florence

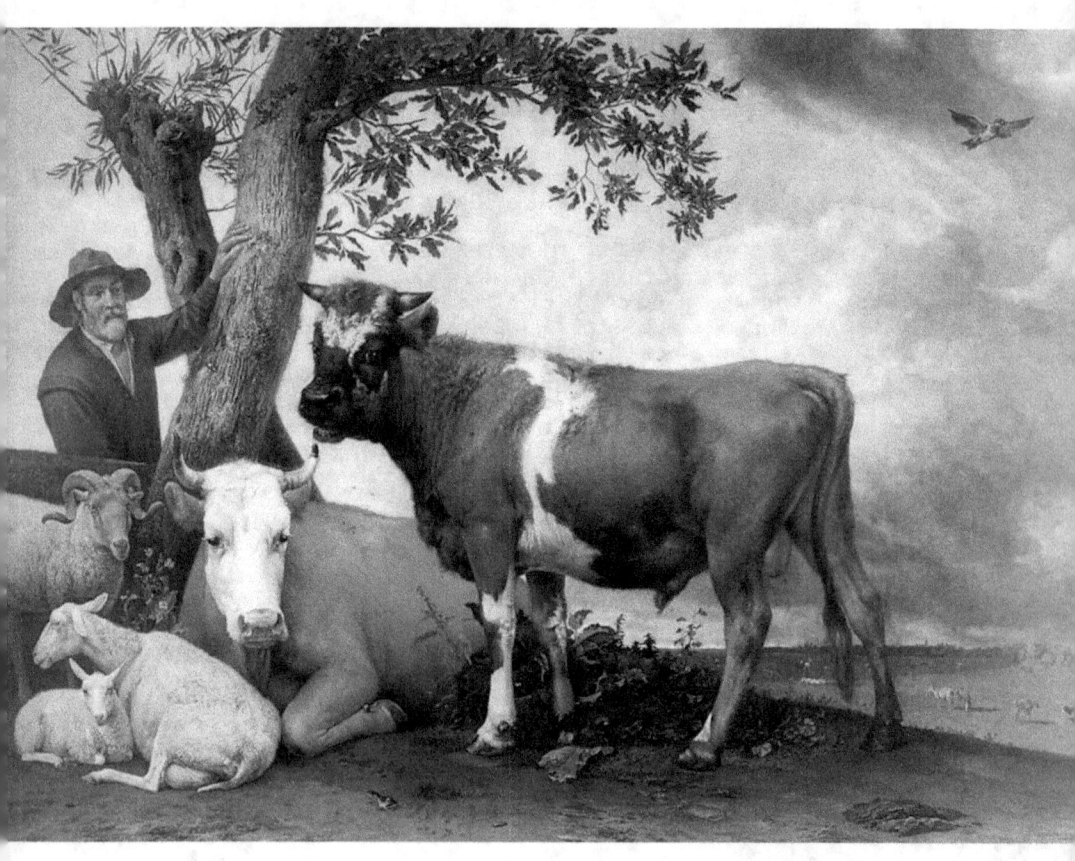

Paulus Potter, Young Bull, 1647, Maritshuis, The Hague

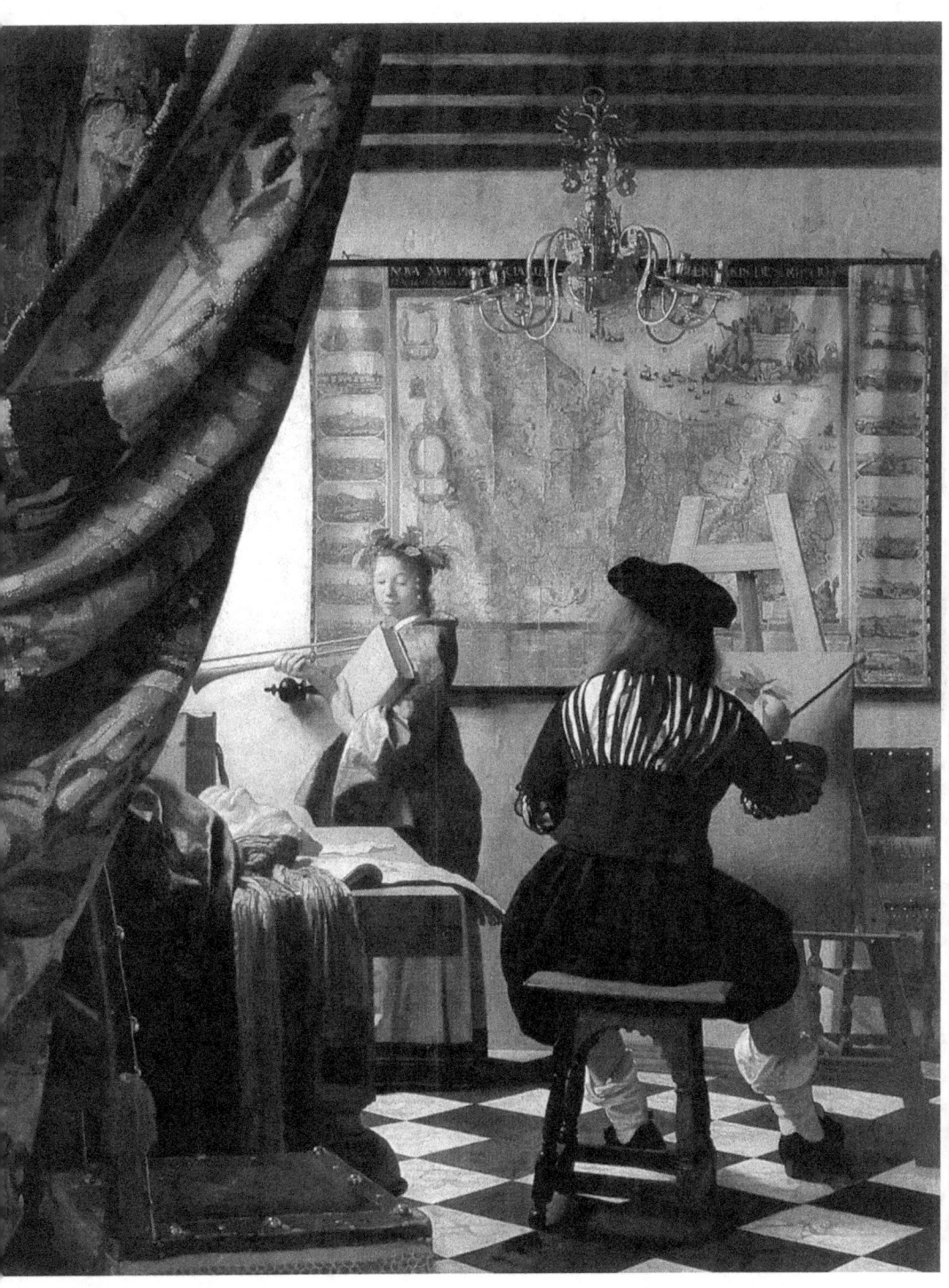

Jan Vermeer, The Allegory of Painting, 1666-67, Kunsthistoriches Museum, Vienna

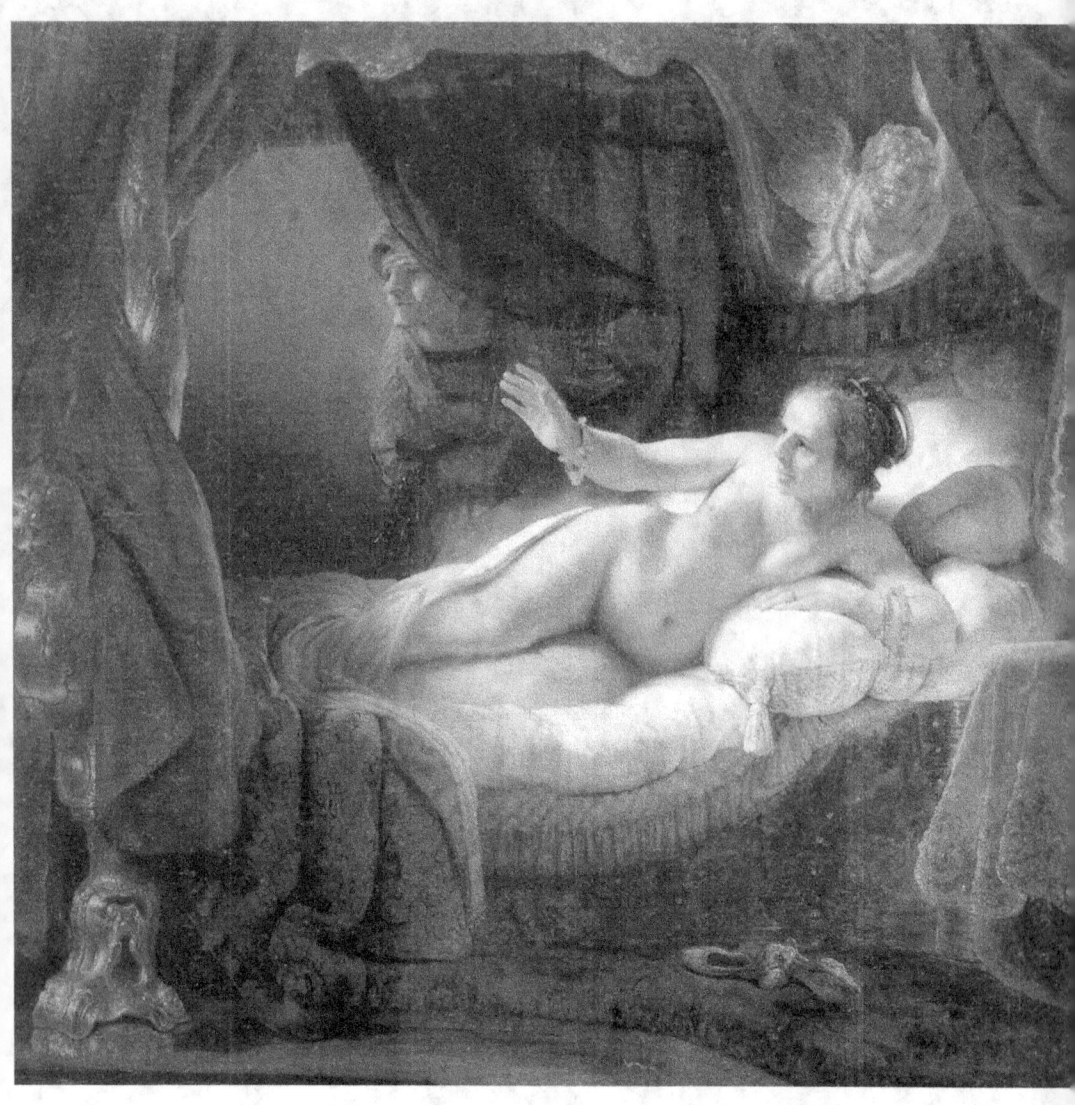

Rembrandt van Rijn, Danae, 1636, St Petersburg

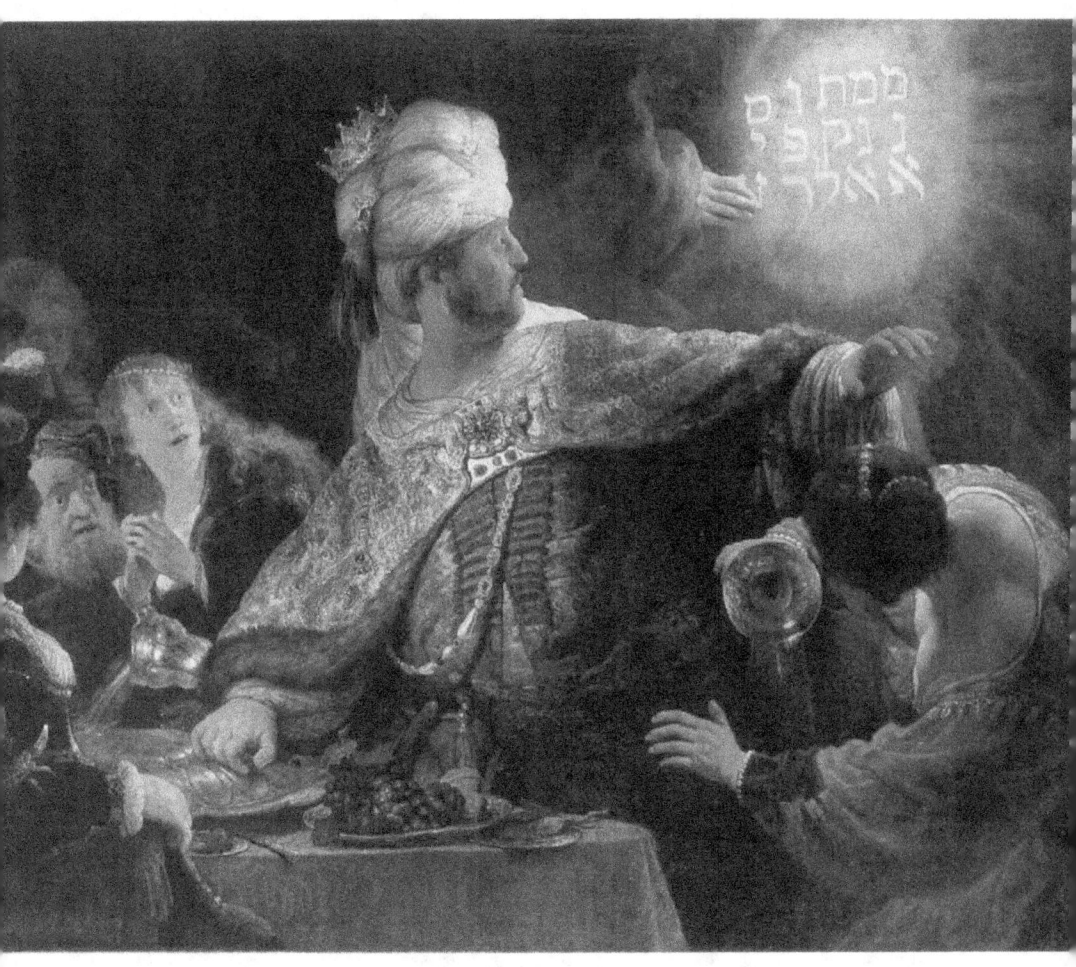

Rembrandt van Rijn, Belshazzar's Feast, 1635, National Gallery, London

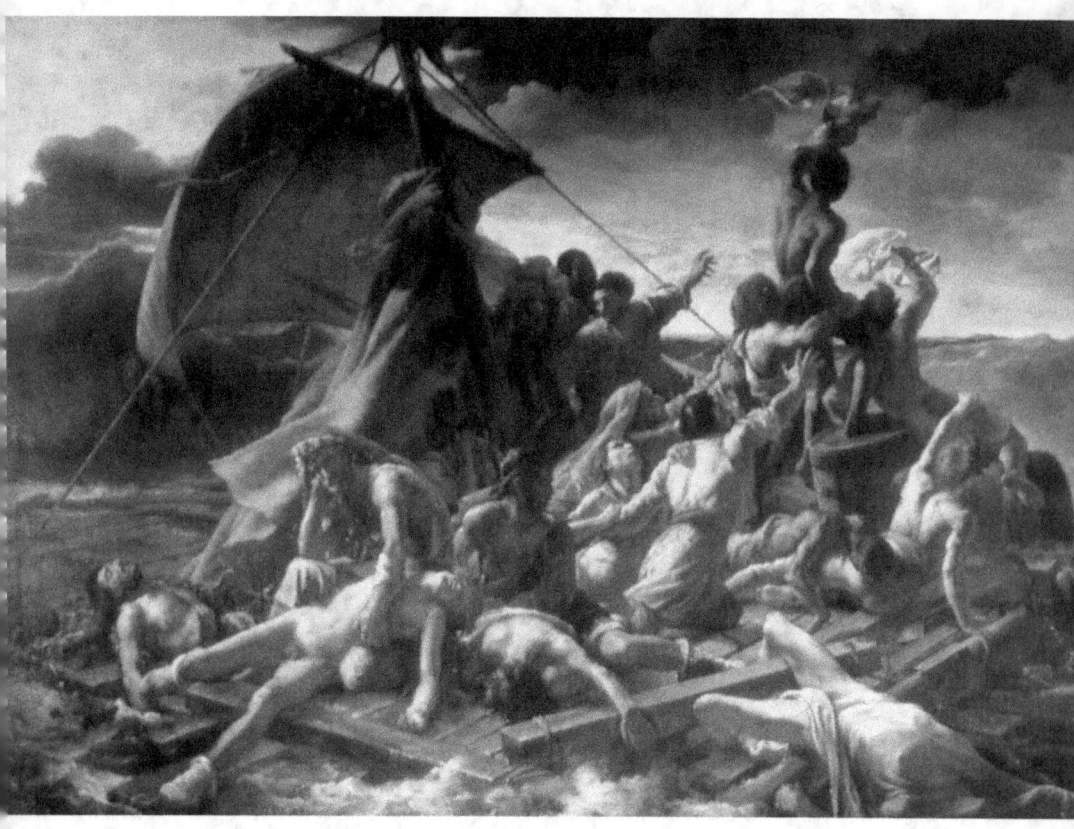

Théodore Géricault, The Raft of the Medusa, 1818-19, Louvre, Paris

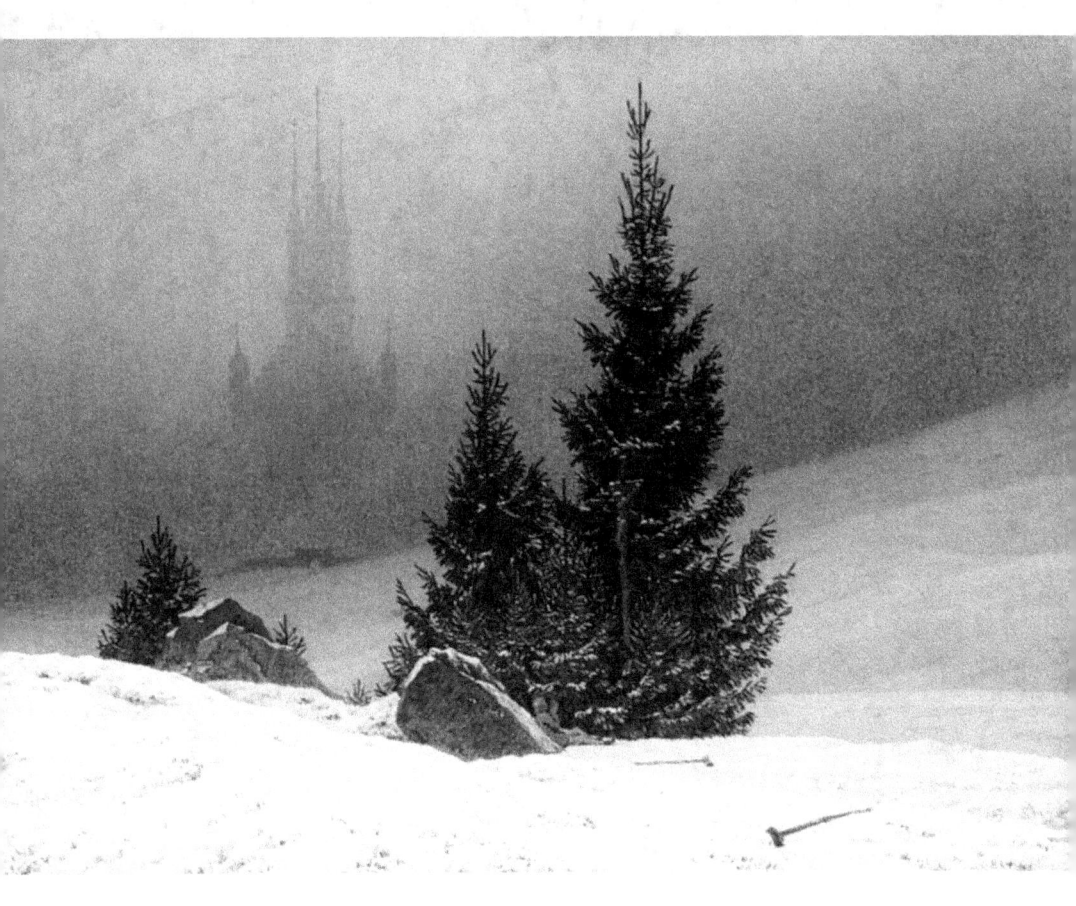

Casper David Friedrich, Winter Landscape, 1811, National Gallery, London

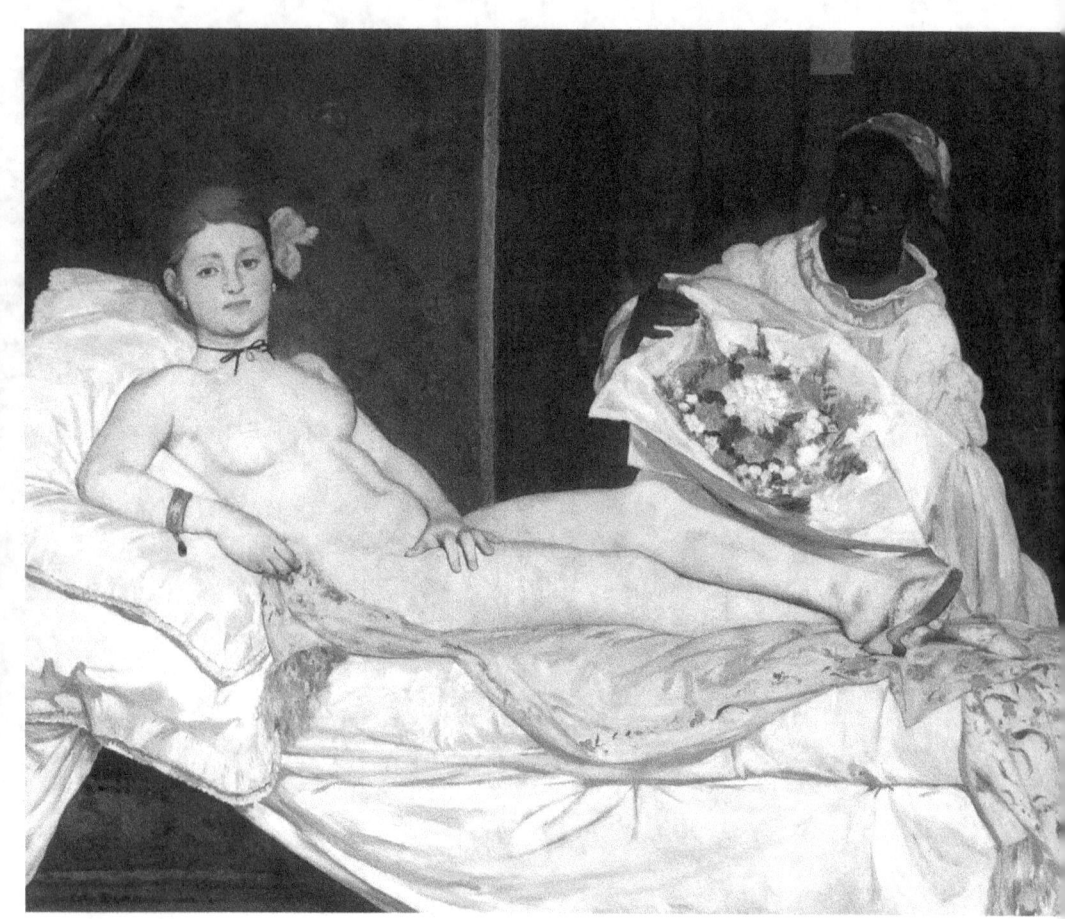

Edouard Manet, Olympia, Musée d'Orsay, Paris

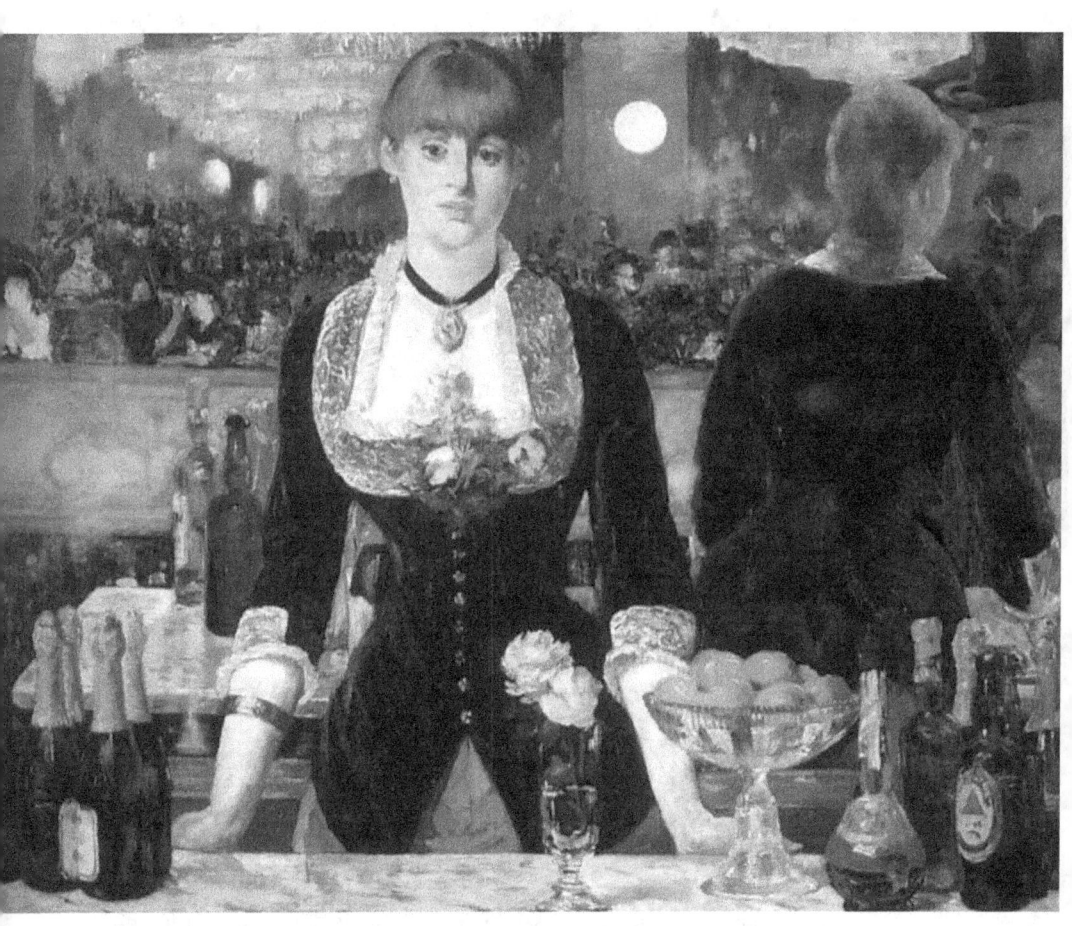

Edouard Manet, Bar at the Folies-Bergères, 1882,Courtauld Institute, London

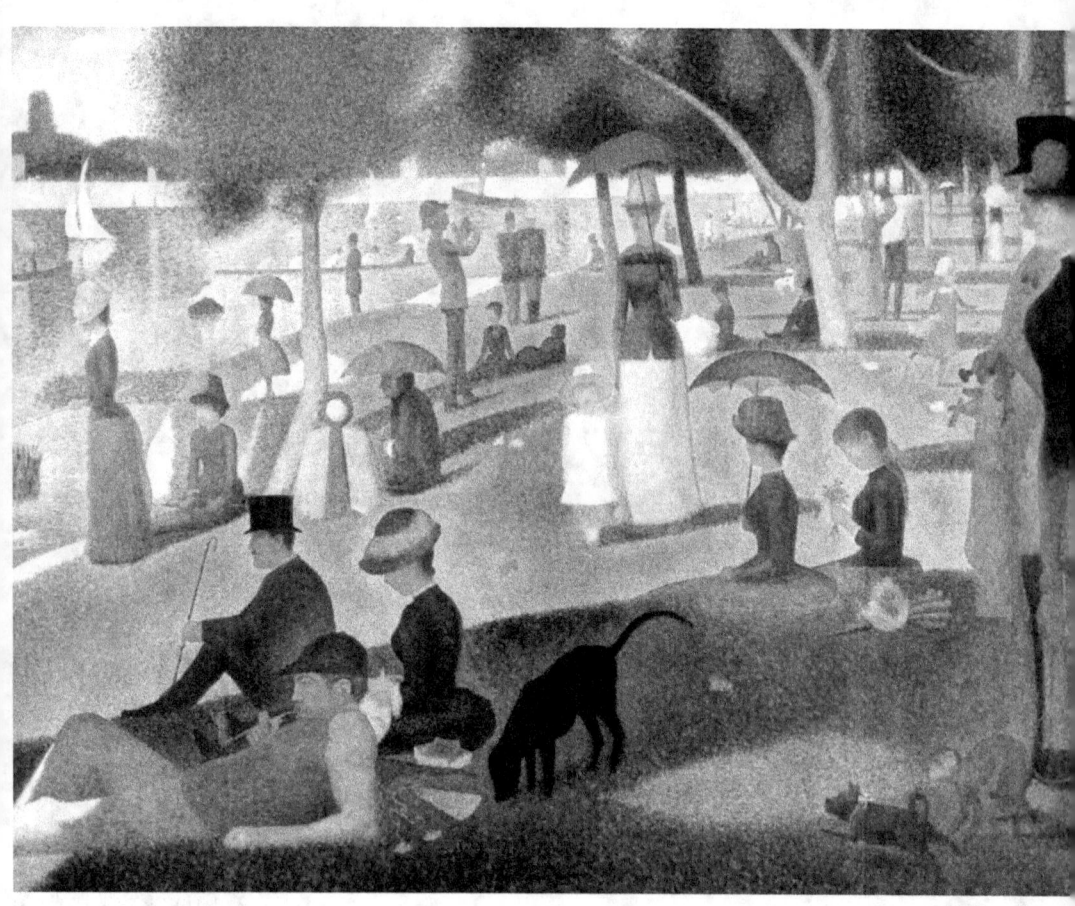

Georges Seurat, Sunday Afternoon On the Island of Grand Jatte, 1884-86
Art Institute, Chicago

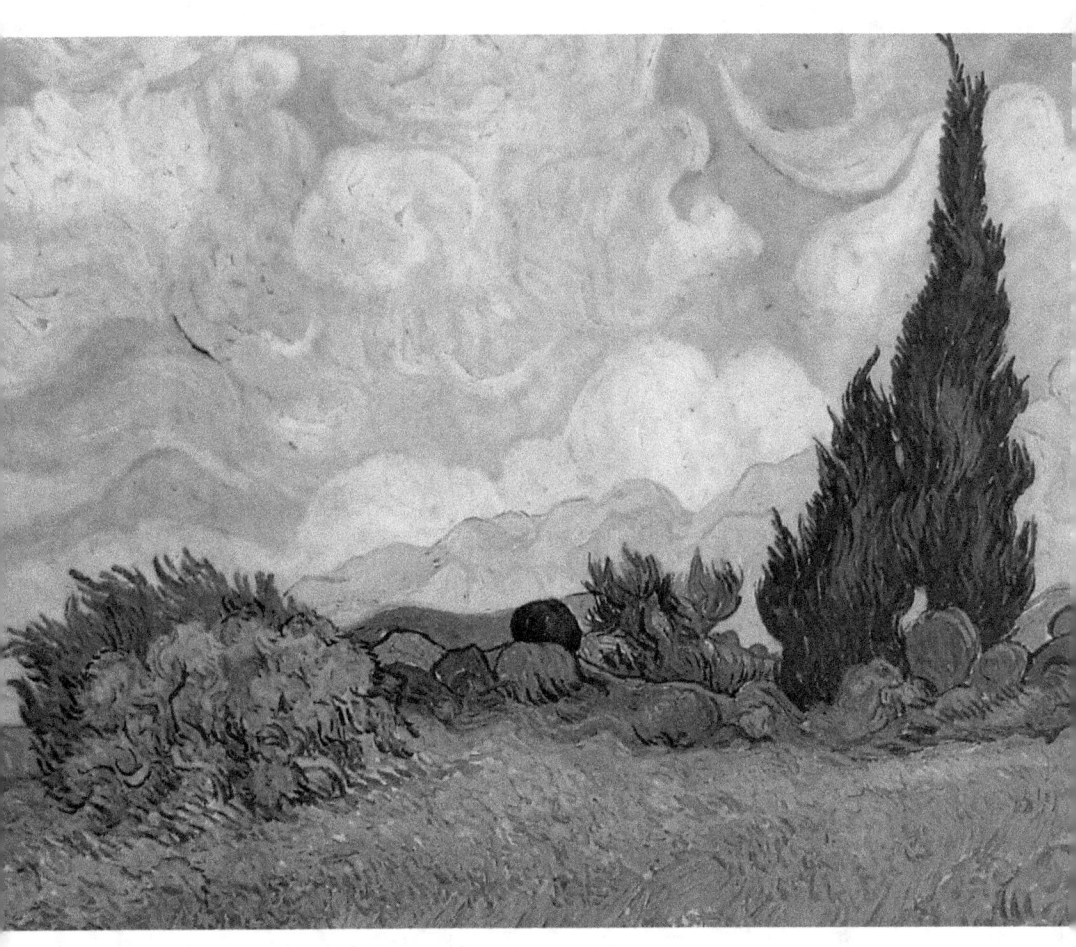

Vincent van Gogh, Wheatfield, Zurich

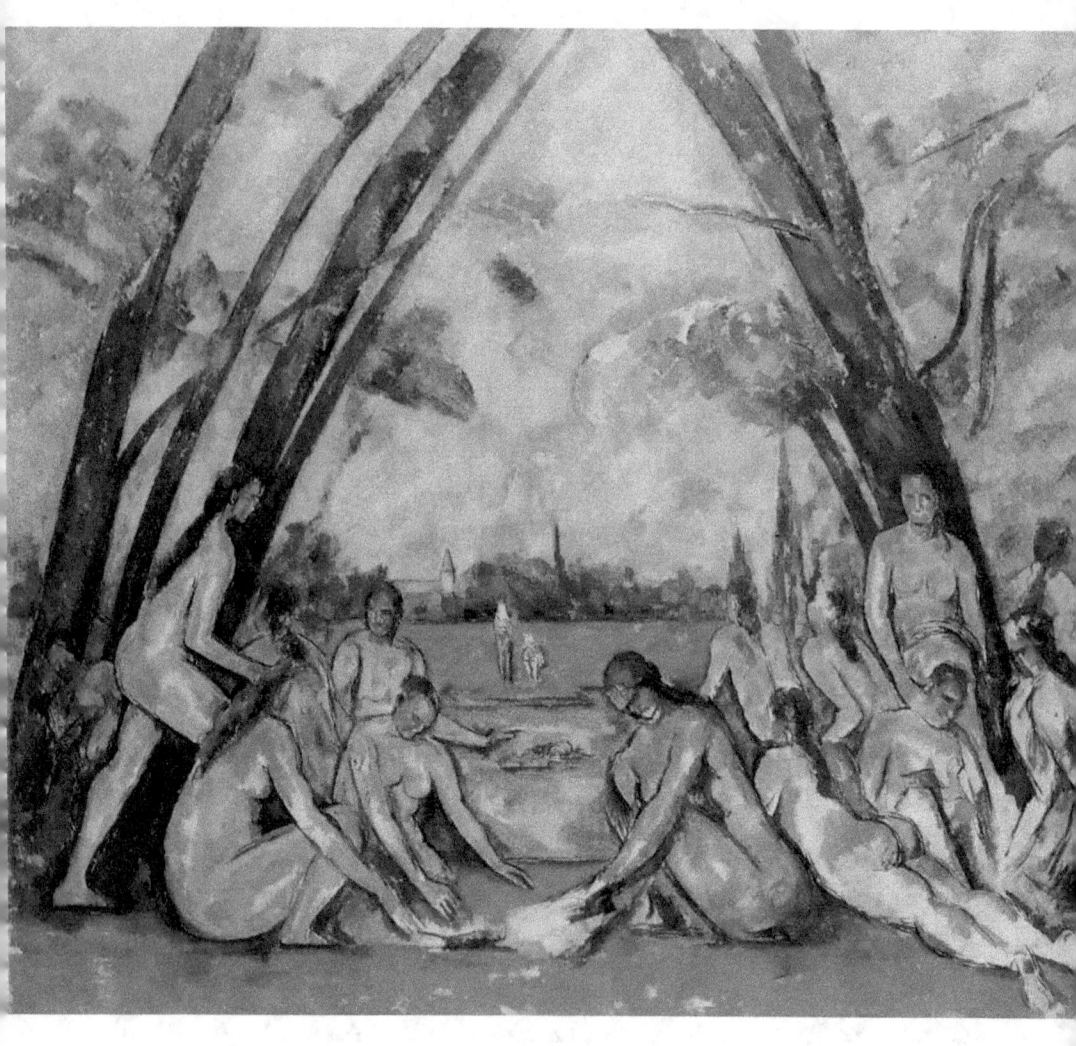

Paul Cézanne, Large Bathers, 1906,
Philadelphia Museum of Art

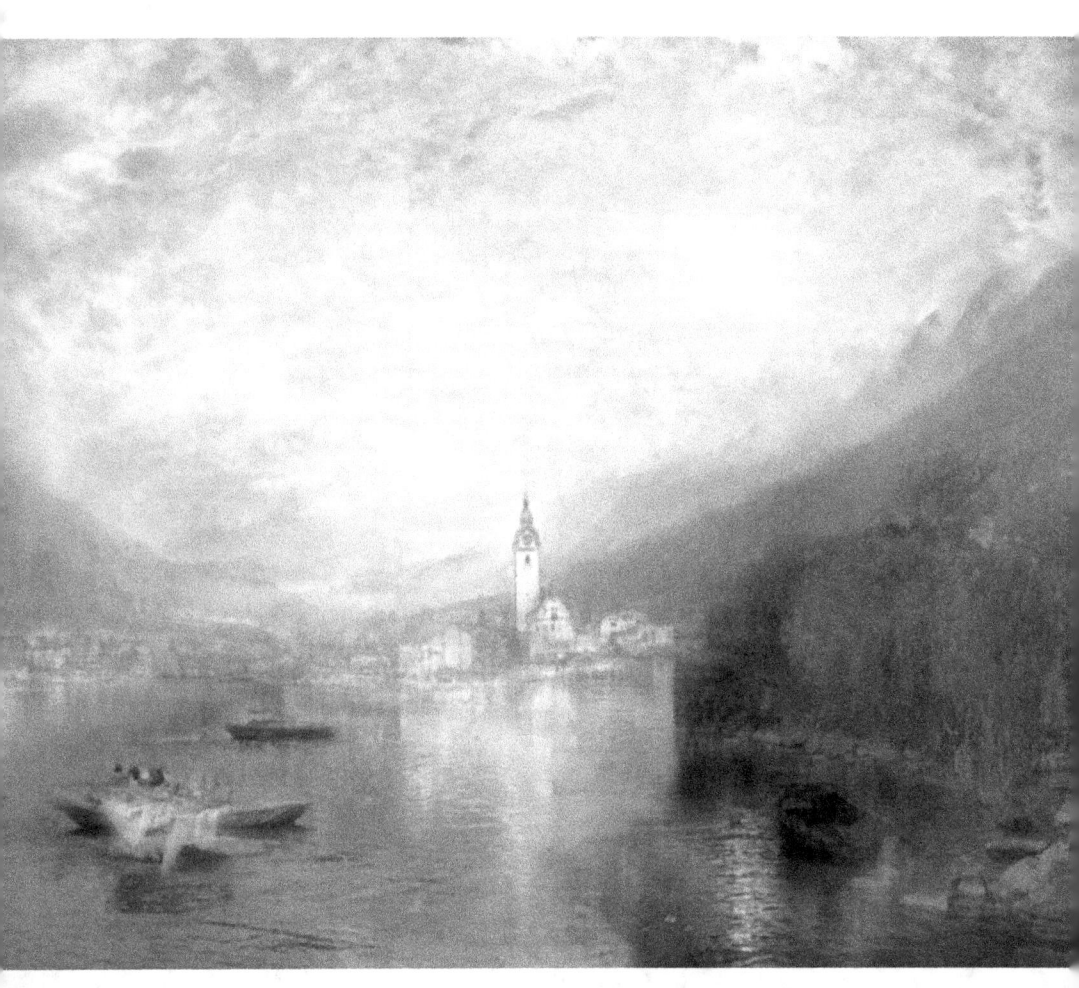

J.M.W. Turner, Lake of Lucerne, Clore Gallery, London

Kasimir Malevich, Suprematist Composition: White On White, 1918,
Museum of Modern Art, New York

Quotes By Frank Stella

I don't like to say I have given my life to art. I prefer to say art has given me my life.

•

One learns about painting by looking at and imitating other painters.

•

You see what you know!

•

People say that the paintings are always big because they're striving for effect, but they're also big so that I don't trip over myself, so that I have room to work, and people can come in and be comfortable.

•

Architecture can't fully represent the chaos and turmoil that are part of the human personality, but you need to put some of that turmoil into the architecture, or it isn't real.

•

I don't like a lot of the stuff that goes on in the art world, but it's hard to be old and like what goes on around you.

The idea that they know what minimalism is is absurd. I don't know what minimalism is!

•

When I'm painting the picture, I'm really painting a picture. I may have a flatfooted technique, or something like that, but still, to me, the thrill, or the meat of the thing, is the actual painting. I don't get any thrill out of laying it out.

•

Abstract paintings must be as real as those created by the 16th century Italians.

•

I always get into arguments with people who want to retain the old values in painting – the humanistic values that they... find on the canvas. If you pin them down, they always end up asserting that there is something there besides the paint on the canvas. My painting is based on the fact that only what can be seen there is there... What you see is what you get.

•

No art is any good unless you can feel how it's put together. By and large it's the eye, the hand and if it's any good, you feel the body. Most of the best stuff seems to be a complete gesture, the totality of the artist's body; you can really lean on it.

•

Up until 35 I had a slightly skewed world view. I honestly believed everybody in the world wanted to make abstract paintings, and people only became lawyers and doctors and brokers and things because they couldn't make abstract paintings

•

I was worried in the 80s that the best abstract painting had become obsessed with materiality, and painterly gestures and materiality were up against the wall.

•

Remember that the 60s was up against the best American art

that anyone had produced, and probably the best international art of the 20th century, minus Picasso and Matisse. But who was going to be as good as Barnett Newman and Clyfford Still? Maybe we weren't, but there was a lot of variety and a lot of trying.

•

I want to make exalted art. A successful image has pictorial lift. I am looking for whatever is up there.

•

A sculpture is just a painting cut out and stood up somewhere.

•

But, after all, the aim of art is to create space – space that is not compromised by decoration or illustration, space within which the subjects of painting can live.

•

I don't know how I got into sculpture. I liked its physicality, that's the only reason.

•

The paintings got sculptural because the forms got more complicated. I've learned to weave in and out.

•

The whole idea of making art is to be open, to be generous, and absorb the viewer and absorb yourself, to let them go into it. I have to go into all those places in order to make it work.

•

I know what I want, but it's physically beyond me now. I can work on what I can handle. It's a playoff between the object and my physical limits.

•

I hate to say this…it's made to order. Then, I disorder it a little bit or, I should say, I reorder it. I wouldn't be so presumptuous to claim that I had the ability to disorder it. I wish I did.

•

What you see is what you see.

Time is what you have left... you just march with it and use it the best you can.

Bibliography

William C. Agee. *Donald Judd*, Whitney Museum of American Art, New York, NY, 1968

—. *The Sculpture of Donald Judd*, Art Museum of South Texas, Corpus Christi, 1977

Lawrence Alloway. "Residual Sign Systems in Abstract Expressionism", *Artforum*, November, 1973

Carl Andre. "Frank Stella: Preface to Stripe Painting", in D. Miller, 1959

D. Anfam. *Abstract Expressionism*, Thames & Hudson, 1990

Emile de Antonio & Mitch Tuchman. *Painters Painting*, Abbeville Press, New York, NY, 1984

M. Archer. *Art Since 1960*, Thames & Hudson, 1997

Isobel Armstrong, ed. *New Feminist Discourses: Critical Essays on Theories and Texts*, Routledge, 1992

Dore Ashton. *American Art Since 1945*, Thames & Hudson, 1982

Richard Axsom. *The Prints of Frank Stella*, University Press, Ann Arbor, 1983

—. *Frank Stella: The Circuits Prints*, Walker Art Center Press, Minneapolis, 1988

Jo Baer. "Letters", *Artforum*, vol. 6, no. 1, September, 1967

E. Baker. "Frank Stella's Perspectives", *Art News*, May, 1970

Gregory Battock, ed. *Minimal Art: A Critical Anthology*, Studio Vista, 1969

S. Beckett. *Collected Shorter Prose 1945-1980*, Calder, 1984

—. *Nohow On*, Calder, 1992

Maurice Berger. *Labyrinths: Robert Morris, Minimalism and the 1960s,* Harper & Row, New York, NY, 1989

Mel Bochner: "Systematic", *Arts Magazine,* vol. 41, no. 1, November, 1966

—. "Serial Art Systems: Solipsism", *Arts Magazine,* vol. 41, no. 8, Summer 1967

D. Bourdon. *Carl Andre: Sculpture 1959-1977,* Jaap Rietman, New York, NY, 1978

Nicolas & Elena Calas. *Icons and Image of the Sixties,* Dutton, New York, NY, 1971

Frederick Castle. "What's That, the '68 Stella? Wow!", *Art News,* 66, 9, January, 1968

Herschel B. Chipp, ed. *Theories of Modern Art,* University Press of California, Los Angeles, 1968

Ronny Cohen. "Frank Stella", *ART News,* May, 1985

Frances Colpitt. *Minimal Art: The Critical Perspective,* University of Washington Press, Seattle, 1990

J.H. Cone. "Frank Stella's New Paintings", *Artforum,* Dec, 1967

Harry Cooper and Megan Luke. *Frank Stella, 1958,* 2006

J. Coplans. "Post-Painterly Abstraction", *Artforum,* 2, 12, Summer, 1964

—. "Serial Imagery", *Artforum,* 7, 2, October, 1968

R. Creeley. "Frank Stella", *Lugano Review,* Summer, 1965

M. Crichton. *Jasper Johns,* Thames & Hudson, 1977

C. Curtis. "Frank Stella and Art", *The New York Times,* 17 March, 1984

Jean-Luc Daval. *History of Abstract Painting,* Art Data, 1989

Willis Domingo. "The Intuition of Form", *Arts Magazine,* 47, 4, February, 1973

P. Dormer. "Frank Stella Paintings as Tapestry", *Apollo,* February, 1989

J. Elderfield. *Morris Louis,* MOMA, New York, NY, 1986

—. *Helen Frankenthaler,* New York, NY, 1989

Franz Fedier. *Frank Stella: Werke 1958-1976,* Kunsthalle Bielfeld, 1977

Lois Finkelstein. "Seeing Stella", *Artforum,* June, 1973

B. Forgey. "Starring Stella", *Washington Star News,* 23 November, 1973

—. "The Charisma of Frank Stella", *Washington Star,* 21 April, 1979

C. Fox. "More in Common Than Meets the Eye in Stella, Freud Retrospective", *Atlanta Constitution,* 18 October, 1987

Noel Frackman. "Tracking Frank Stella's Circuit Series", *Arts,* April, 1982

—. "Frank Stella's Abstract Expressionist Aerie: A Reading of Stella's New Paintings", *Arts,* December, 1976

Richard Francis. *Jasper Johns,* New York, NY, 1984

M. Fried. "New York Letter", *Art International,* vol. 8, no. 3, April, 1964

—. *Three American Painters: Kenneth Noland, Jules Olitski, Frank Stella,* Fogg Art Museum, Harvard University, Cambridge, Mass., 1965

—. "Shape as Form: Frank Stella's New Paintings", *Artforum*, 5, 3, November, 1966

—. *Frank Stella*, Pasadena Art Museum, 1966

—. "Art and Objecthood", *Artforum*, 5, Summer, 1967

Alan Friedman. "Frank Stella: Pop Versus Pagan", *M*, June, 1992

P. Fuller. *Peter Fuller's Modern Painters: Reflections on British Art*, ed. J. McDonald, Methuen, 1993

D. Galloway. "Stella's Deep-Dish Pie", *International*, February, 1993

C. Geelhaar. *Frank Stella Workings Drawings 1956-1970*, tr. C. Hamlin, Kunstmuseum, Basel, 1980

Bruce Glaser. "Questions to Stella and Judd"," ed. Lucy Lippard, *Art News*, 65, 5, September, 1966

Grace Glueck. "Art: Frank Stella's Prints at the Whitney", *The New York Times*, 14 January, 1983

Paul Goldberger. *Frank Stella: Painting into Architecture*, Metropolitan Museum of Art Publications, 2007

Judith Goldman. *Frank Stella*, Princeton University Museum of Art, 1983

R. Goldwater & Marco Treves, eds. *Artists on Art*, John Murray, 1975

Clement Greenberg. "Modernist Painting", *Arts Yearbook*, 4, Art Digest, New York, NY, 1961

—. *Post-Painterly Abstraction*, Los Angeles County Museum, Los Angeles, 1964

Sidney Guberman. *Frank Stella: An Illustrated Biography* Rizzoli, New York, NY, 1995

P. Halley. "Frank Stella and the Simulacrum", *Flash Art*, Feb-March, 1986

E. Heartney. "Frank Stella at 65 Thompson", *Art in America*, June, 1991

Thomas Hess. *Barnett Newman*, Walker, New York, NY, 1969

Klaus Honnef. *Contemporary Art*, Benedikt Taschen, Cologne, 1988

Budd Hopkins. "Frank Stella's New Work", *Artforum*, April, 1976

R. Hughes. *Frank Stella: The Swan Engravings*, Forth Worth Art Museum, 1984

—. "The Grand Maximalist", *Time*, 2 November, 1987

Sam Hunter, ed. *An American Renaissance: Painting and Sculpture Since 1940*, Abbeville Press, New York, NY, 1986

—. *American Art of the 20th Century*, Thames & Hudson, 1973

Waldemar Januszczak, ed. *Techniques of the World's Great Painters*, Phaidon, 1980

Donald Judd. "Frank Stella", *Arts Magazine*, 36, Sept, 1962

—. "In the Galleries", *Arts Magazine*, vol. 37, no. 10, September, 1963, 55

—. "Local History", *Arts Yearbook 7*, 1964

—. "Specific Objects", *Arts Yearbook*, 8, 1965

—. "Black, White and Gray", *Arts Magazine*, 38, 6, Mch, 1964

—. "Barnett Newman", *Studio International*, 179, 919, Feb, 1970

—. *Complete Writings, 1959-1975*, Nova Scotia College of Art and Design, Halifax, Canada, 1975

—. *Complete Writings, 1975-1986*, Van Abbemuseum, Netherlands, 1987

Brian P. Kennedy. *Frank Stella: Irregular Polygons, 1965-66*, 2011

Roger Kimball. "Frank Stella", *The New Criterion*, December, 1987

Max Kozloff. "Pop Culture, Metaphysical Designs and the New Vulgarians", *Art International*, March, 1962

—. "New York Letter", *Art International*, 8, 3, April, 1964

—. *Jasper Johns*, New York, NY, 1969

H. Kramer. "Frank Stella Retrospective at the Modern", *The New York Observer*, 19 October, 1987

Rosalind E. Krauss. *Passages in Modern Sculpture*, Thames & Hudson, 1977

Donald Kuspit. "Authoritarian Abstraction", *Journal of Aesthetics and Art Criticism*, 36, 1, Autumn, 1977

Kay Larson. "Stella Performance", *New York Magazine*, 26 October, 1987

Philip Leider. "Literalism and Abstraction: Frank Stella's Retrospective at the Modern", *Artforum*, 8, April, 1970

—. "Shakespeare's Fish", *Art in America*, Oct, 1990

—. *Stella Since 1970*, Fort Worth Art Museum, Texas, 1978

Lucy Lippard. "An Impure Situation", *Art International*, 20 May, 1966a

—. "New York Letter: Recent Sculpture as Escape", *Art International*, Feb, 1966b

—. "Escalataion in Washington", *Art International*, vol. 12, no. 1, January, 1968

—. *From the Center: feminist essays on women's art*, Dutton, New York, NY, 1976

—. *Ad Reinhardt*, Abrams, New York, NY, 1981

—. *Six Years: The Dematerialization of the Art Object from 1966 to 1972*, Praeger, New York, NY, 1973

Edward Lucie-Smith. *Art Today*, Phaidon, 1989

J. McLean. *Frank Stella*, Hayward Gallery, 1970

Kynaston McShine. *Primary Structures*, Jewish Museum, New York, NY, 1966

James Mellow. "New York Letter", *Art International*, 20 April, 1966

Franz Meyer. *Frank Stella*, Kunstahlle, Basel, 1976

Dorothy C. Miller, ed. *Sixteen Americans*, MOMA, New York, NY, 1959

M. Moorman. "Frank Stella", *ART News*, Summer, 1989

R. Morris. "Notes on Sculpture", part 3, *Artforum* 5, 10, Summer, 1967

Lynda Nead. *Female Nude: Art, Obscenity and Sexuality*, Routledge, 1992

Sheldon Nodelman. *Marden, Novros, Rothko: Painting in the Age of Actuality*, Institute for the Arts, Rice University, Houston, 1978

—. "Sixties Art: Some Philosophical Perspectives", *Perspecta: The Yale*

Architectural Journal, 11, 1967

Brian O'Doherty. "Frank Stella and a Crisis of Nothingness", *New York Times*, 19 January 1964, section 2, 21

Fred Orton. *Jasper Johns: The Sculptures*, Henry Moore Institute, Leeds, 1996

A. Pacquement. *Frank Stella*, Flammarion, Paris, 1988

Andreas C. Papadakis, ed. *The New Romantics*, Art & Design (4, 11/12), Academy Group, 1988

—. ed. *British and American Art: The Uneasy Dialectic*, Art & Design (3, 9/10), Academy Group, 1987

—. ed. *Abstract Art and the Rediscovery of the Spiritual*, Art & Design (3, 5/6), Academy Group, 1987

Jeff Perrone. "Review", *Artforum*, December, 1976

B. Peters. "Behind Closed Doors: Frank Stella", *Met Home*, July, 1993

R. Pincus-Witten. "Systematic Painting", *Artforum*, 5, 3, November, 1966

—. *Postminimalism*, Out of London, New York, NY, 1977

Carter Ratcliff. *In the Realm of the Monochrome*, Renaissance Society, University of Chicago, Chicago, 1979

—. "Frank Stella: Portrait of the Artist as an Image Administrator", *Art in America*, 73, 2, February, 1985

—. "Mostly Monochrome", *Art in America*, 69, 4, April, 1981

V. Raynor. "Frank Stella: Portraits of His Alma Mater", *The New York Times*, 7 November, 1982

Ad Reinhardt. *Art as Art: The Selected Writings of Ad Reinhardt*, University of California Press, Berkeley, 1991

B. Reinhardt *et al. Frank Stella, Moby Dick Series*, Ulmer Museum, 1993

R. Reiss. "Frank Stella '58", *Princeton Alumni Weekly*, 11 June, 1979

Paul Richard. "Stella: Not So Simple Anymore", *Washington Post*, 10 November, 1973

Brenda Richardson. *Frank Stella: The Black Paintings*, Baltimore Museum of Art, Baltimore, 1976

Charles A. Riley II. *Color Codes: Modern Theories in Color in Philosophy, Painting and Architecture, Literature, Music and Psychology*, University Press of New England, Hanover, 1995

P. Rinzler. "Frank Stella, a 17-Year Retrospective", *Splash*, Winter, 1987

Corinne Robins, ed. *The Pluralist Era: American Art 1968-1981*, Harper & Row, New York, NY, 1984

Barbara Rose. *American Art Since 1900*, Thames & Hudson, 1967

—. *American Painting*, Skira/ Rizzoli, New York, NY, 1986

—. "ABC Art", *Art in America*, 53, 5, November, 1965

R. Rosenblum. *Modern Painting and the Northern Romantic Tradition*, Thames & Hudson, 1978

—. *Jasper Johns' Paintings and Sculptures 1954-1974*, Ann Arbor, Michigan, 1985

—. *Frank Stella*, Penguin, 1971

—. "Frank Stella: Five Years of Variations on an Irreducible Theme", *Artforum*, 3, 6, March, 1965

Stephanie Rosenthal. *Black Paintings: Robert Rauschenberg, Ad Reinhardt, Mark Rothko, Frank Stella*, 2007

Lawrence Rubin. *Frank Stella Paintings: 1958-1965*, New York, NY, 1986

William S. Rubin. *Frank Stella*, New York Graphic Society, Greenwich, Conn., 1970

—. *Frank Stella: 1970-1987*, MOMA, New York, NY, 1987

J. Russell. "The Power of Frank Stella", *The New York Times*, 1 February, 1985

—. "The Risky Works From Stella at the Museum of Modern Art", *The New York Times*, 16 October, 1987

Irwin Sandler. "The New Cool-Art", *Art in America*, 53, 1, February, 1965

—. *The Triumph of American Painting*, Harper & Row, 1970

—. *American Art of the 1960s*, Harper & Row, New York, 1988

—. *Art of the Postmodern Era: From the 1960s to the Early 1990s*, Harper-Collins, 1997

B. Schwabsky. "Frank Stella", *Arts Magazine*, April, 1991

W. Seitz. *Recent Paintings of Frank Stella*, Rose Art Museum, 1969

D. Shapiro & Cecil Shapiro, eds. *Abstract Expressionism: A Critical Record*, Cambridge University Press, 1990

R. Smith. "Frank Stella's New Paintings", *Art in America*, December, 1975

—. "Schnabel and Stella", *The New York Times*, 6 December, 1987

—. "Frank Stella's New Direction", *The New York Times*, 21 October, 1994

Naomi Spector. *Robert Ryman,* Whitechapel Art Gallery, 1977

Nikos Stangos, ed. *Concepts of Modern Art*, Thames & Hudson, 1981

Frank Stella. *Working Space*, Harvard University Press, Cambridge, Mass., 1986 [abbr. as WS]

—. *Conversations with Frank Stella*, ed. Devolder, Editions Tandem, 1994

S. Stephens. "Portrait: Frank Stella, Blurring the Line Between Art and Architecture", *Architectural Digest*, July, 1994

Kristine Stiles & P. Selz, eds. *Theories & Documents of Contemporary Art: A Sourcebook of Artists' Writings*, University of California Press, Berkeley, 1996

R. Storr. "Frank Stella's Norton Lectures: A Response", *Art in America*, February, 1985

C. Tomkins. "Profiles", *New Yorker*, Sept, 1984

Maurice Tuchman. *The New York School*, Thames & Hudson, 1971

—. *The Spiritual in Art: Abstract Painting 1880-1985*, Los Angeles County Museum of Art/ Abbeville Press, New York, NY, 1986

Samuel Wagstaff. "Paintings to Think About", *Art News*, vol. 62, no. 9,

January, 1964

Diane Waldman. *Carl Andre,* Guggenheim, New York, NY, 1970

—. *Robert Ryman,* New York, NY, 1972

—. "Color, Format and Abstract Art: An Interview with Kenneth Noland", *Art in America,* 65, 3, May, 1977

—. *Mark Rothko,* Thames & Hudson, 1978

L. Weschler. "Stella's Flying Ships", *Art News,* Sept, 1987

C. Wheeler. "Frank Stella: Reassuringly Expensive?", *The Independent,* 10 July, 1990

Daniel Wheeler. *Art Since Mid-Century: 1945 to the Present,* Thames & Hudson, 1991

W. Wilson. "Frank Stella: Minimalist to the Max", *Los Angeles Times,* 4 June, 1989

Ann Sargent Wooster: "Sol LeWitt's Expanding Grid", *Art in America,* vol. 68, no. 5, May, 1980

Some Works Cited

La Vecchia dell' Orto, 1986, mixed media, Musée national d'art moderne, Paris

Guadalupe Island Caracara, 1979, mixed media on honeycomb and sandwich foam aluminium, 93.8 x 121 x 18 in, Tate Modern, London

Diavolozoppo, 1984, oil, urethane enamel, fluorescent alkyd, acrylic, and printing ink on canvas, etched magnesium, aluminium and fibreglass, 139 x 170 x 16in, collection: the artist

Thruxton 3X, 1982, mixed media on etched aluminium, 75 x 85 x 15 in, Shindler Collection, Honolulu

Hyena Stomp, 1962, acrylic on canvas, 77 x 77 in, Tate Modern, London

Reiher in der Bonninacht no. 1, 1977, Museum Ludwig, Cologne

Moby Dick, 1989, mixed media, 67.3 x 54.5 in, Waddington's, London

Going Abroad, 1989, hand-coloured collage, with marbling and lithographic, lino and silkscreen printing, 73.4 by 54.7 inches, Waddington's, London

Quathlamba, 1964, metallic powder in polymer emulsion on canvas, 6.4 x 13.6ft, collection: S. Carter, New York, NY

Avicenna, 1960, aluminium paint on canvas, 74.5 x 72in, Menil Collection, Texas

D, 1963, metallic paint on canvas, 6.7 x 7.1ft, collection: Irving Blum

Coney Island, 1958, oil on canvas, Yale University Art Gallery

Warka III, 1973, mixed media, tilted relief, 93 x 100in, collection; the artist

Leblon II, 1975, mixed media on honeycombed aluminium, 80 x 116in, collection: the artist

Point of Pines, 1959, black enamel on canvas, 83.8 x 109.2in, collection: the artist

Tomlinson Court Park, 1959, enamel on canvas, 7.1 x 9.2in, collection: Robert A. Rowan, Pasadena

Maha-lat, 1977, printed metal alloy sheets, wire mesh, and soldered and welded metal scraps with crayon, 15.5 x 20in, MOMA, New York, NY

Shama, 1979, mixed media on aluminium, 78 x 125 x 35.6in, M. Knoedler Gallery, New York, NY

Stellers Albatross, 1976, mixed media on aluminium, 8.6 x 8.2 x 6ft, Saatchi Collection, London

Takht-i-Sulayman, 1967, polymer & fluorescent polymer paint on canvas, 10 x 20ft, Menil Foundation Collection, Houston

Shards, 1983, mixed media on aluminium, 11.3 x 9.9 x 2.1 feet, Leo Castelli Gallery, New York, NY

Corpo-senza-l'anima, 1987, aluminium, 130 x 116 x 59.5in, Galerie Strelow, Düsseldorf

THE ART OF ANDY GOLDSWORTHY

COMPLETE WORKS: SPECIAL EDITION
(PAPERBACK and HARDBACK)

by William Malpas

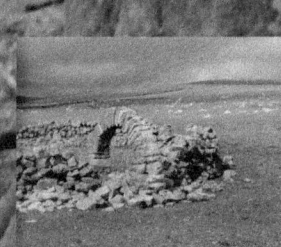 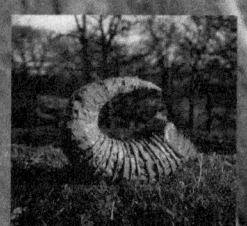

A new, special edition of the study of the contemporary British sculptor, Andy Goldsworthy, including a new introduction, new bibliography and many new illustrations.

This is the most comprehensive, up-to-date, well-researched and in-depth account of Goldsworthy's art available anywhere.

Andy Goldsworthy makes land art. His sculpture is a sensitive, intuitive response to nature, light, time, growth, the seasons and the earth. Goldsworthy's environmental art is becoming ever more popular: 1993's art book *Stone* was a bestseller; the press raved about Goldsworthy taking over a number of London West End art galleries in 1994; during 1995 Goldsworthy designed a set of Royal Mail stamps and had a show at the British Museum. Malpas surveys all of Goldsworthy's art, and analyzes his relation with other land artists such as Robert Smithson, Walter de Maria, Richard Long and David Nash, and his place in the contemporary British art scene.

The Art of Andy Goldsworthy discusses all of Goldsworthy's important and recent exhibitions and books, including the *Sheepfolds* project; the TV documentaries; *Wood* (1996); the New York Holocaust memorial (2003); and Goldsworthy's collaboration on a dance performance.

Illustrations: 70 b/w, 1 colour. 330 pages. New, special, 2nd edition. Publisher: Crescent Moon Publishing. Distributor: Gardners Books.

ISBN 1-86171-059-3 (9781861710598) (Paperback) £25.00 / $44.00

ISBN 1-86171-080-1 (9781861710802) (Hardback) £60.00 / $105.00

ANDY GOLDSWORTHY
IN CLOSE-UP

SPECIAL EDITION (HARDBACK and PAPERBACK)

by William Malpas

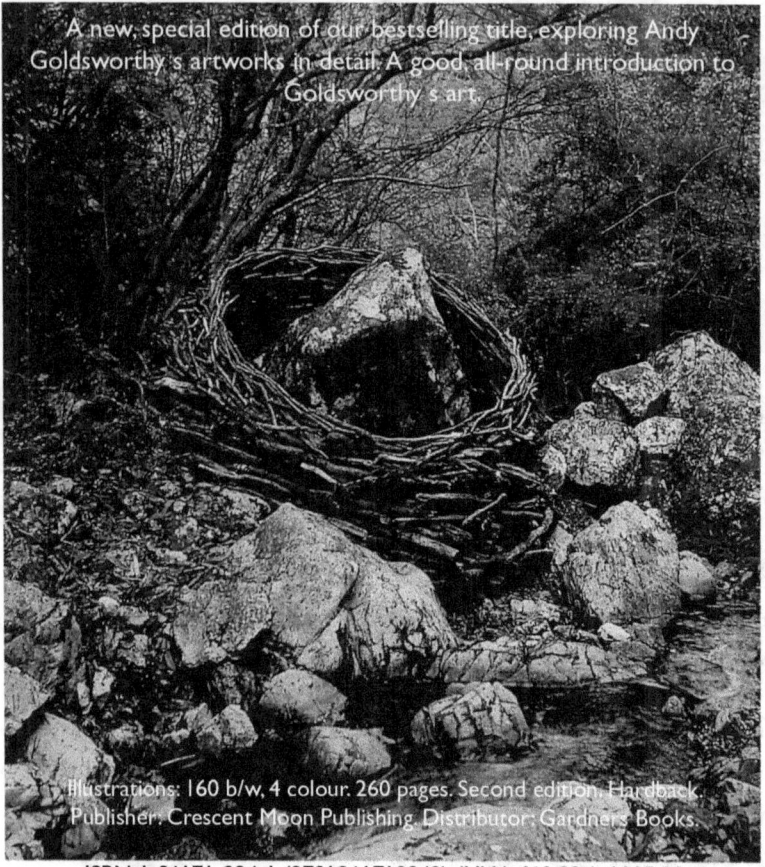

A new, special edition of our bestselling title, exploring Andy
Goldsworthy's artworks in detail. A good, all-round introduction to
Goldsworthy's art.

Illustrations: 160 b/w, 4 colour. 260 pages. Second edition. Hardback.
Publisher: Crescent Moon Publishing. Distributor: Gardners Books.

ISBN 1-86171-094-1 (9781861710949) (Hbk) £60.00 / $105.00

ISBN 1-86171-091-7 (9781861710919) (Pbk) £25.00 / $44.00

Available from bookstores. amazon.com, play.com, tesco.com, and other web-
sites.
In the United States from Baker & Taylor, (800) 7753760 or (800) 7751100
or (908) 5417062. electser@btol.com or btinfo@btol.com.

ANDY GOLDSWORTHY

TOUCHING NATURE:
SPECIAL EDITION

(PAPERBACK and HARDBACK)

by William Malpas

A new, special and updated edition of our bestselling title, providing an excellent general introduction to the art of Andy Goldsworthy.

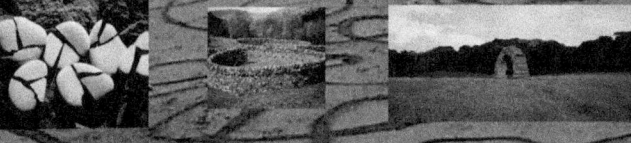

Illustrations: 75 b/w, 2 colour. 354 pages. Third edition. Paperback.

Publisher: Crescent Moon Publishing. Distributor: Gardners Books.

ISBN 1-86171-056-9 (9781861717) (Paperback) £25.00 / $44.00

ISBN 1-86171-087-9 (9781861710871) (Hardback) £60.00 / $105.00

LAND ART

A COMPLETE GUIDE TO LANDSCAPE, ENVIRONMENTAL, EARTHWORKS, NATURE, SCULPTURE AND INSTALLATION ART

by William Malpas

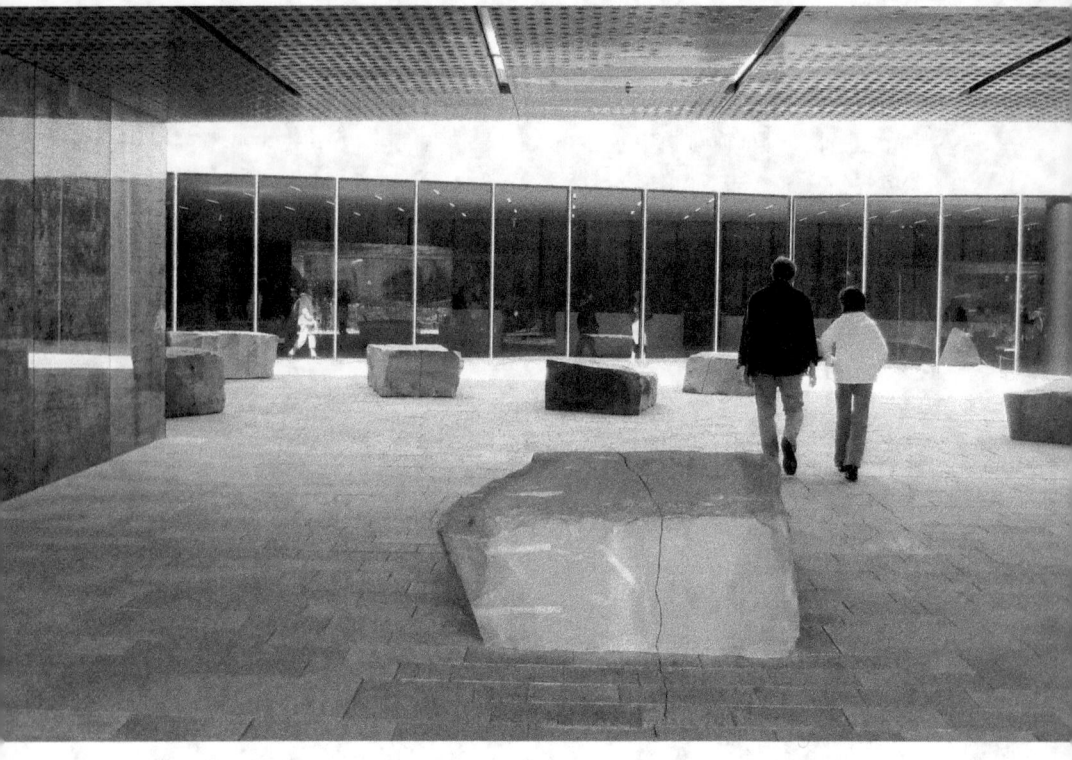

A new, special edition of our popular book on land art.
Chapters on land artists such as Robert Smithson, Walter de Maria, Christo,
Michael Heizer, Richard Long and Andy Goldsworthy.

Illustrations: 35 b/w, 2 colour. 314 pages. First edition. Paperback.

Publisher: Crescent Moon Publishing. Distributor: Gardners Books.

ISBN 1-86171-062-3 (9781861710628) £25.00 / $44.00

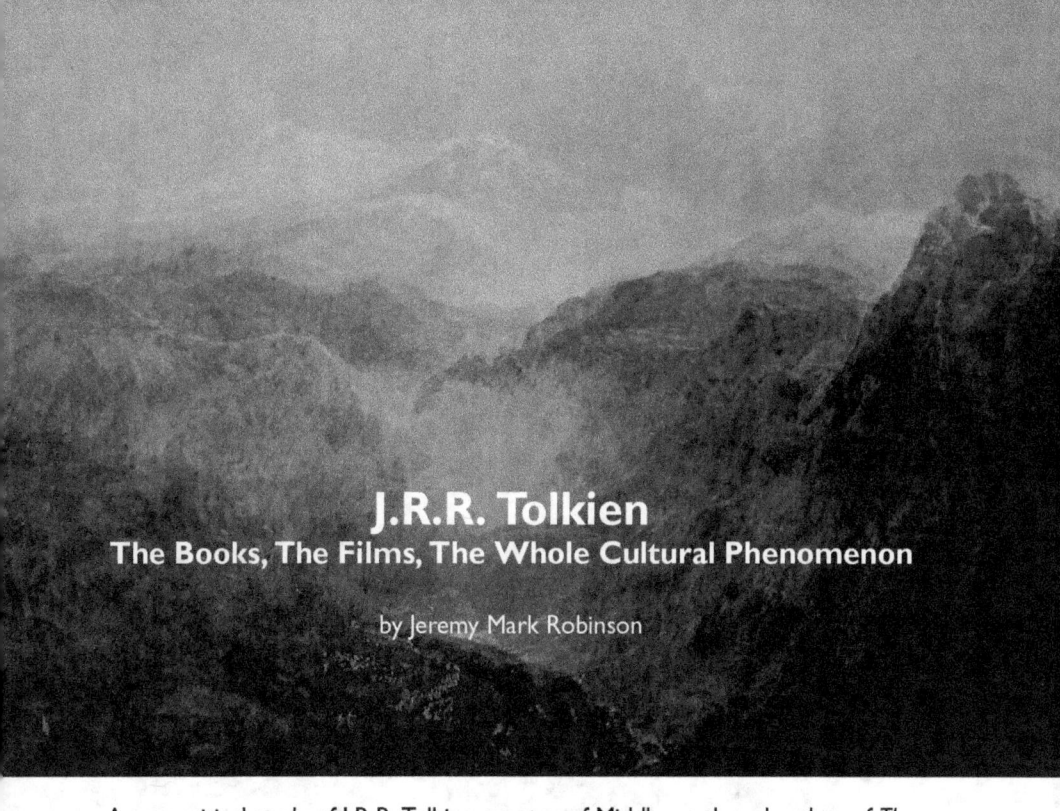

J.R.R. Tolkien
The Books, The Films, The Whole Cultural Phenomenon

by Jeremy Mark Robinson

A new critical study of J.R.R. Tolkien, creator of Middle-earth and author of *The Lord of the Rings, The Hobbit* and *The Silmarillion,* among other books.

This new critical study explores Tolkien's major writings (*The Lord of the Rings, The Hobbit, Beowulf: The Monster and the Critics, The Letters, The Silmarillion* and *The History of Middle-earth* volumes); Tolkien and fairy tales; the mythological, political and religious aspects of Tolkien's Middle-earth; the critics' response to Tolkien's fiction over the decades; the Tolkien industry (merchandizing, toys, role-playing games, posters, Tolkien societies, conferences and the like); Tolkien in visual and fantasy art; the cultural aspects of The Lord of the Rings (from the 1950s to the present); Tolkien's fiction's relationship with other fantasy fiction, such as C.S. Lewis and *Harry Potter;* and the TV, radio and film versions of Tolkien's books, including the 2001-03 Hollywood interpretations of *The Lord of the Rings.*

This new book draws on contemporary cultural theory and analysis and offers a sympathetic and illuminating (and sceptical) account of the Tolkien phenomenon. This book is designed to appeal to the general reader (and viewer) of Tolkien: it is written in a clear, jargon-free and easily-accessible style.

754pp   ISBN 1-86171-057-7   £25.00 / $37.50

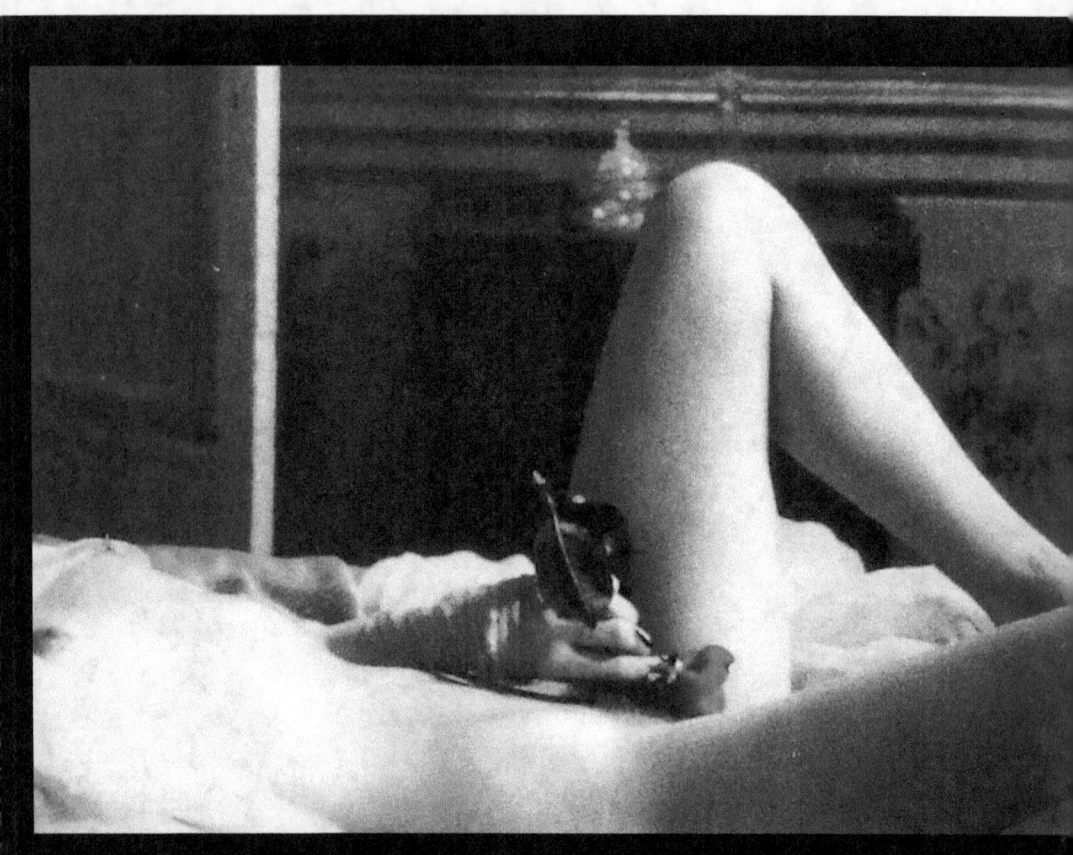

Walerian Borowczyk

Cinema of Erotic Dreams

by Jeremy Mark Robinson

Walerian Borowczyk (1923-2006) was a Polish artist, animator and filmmaker who lived
in France for much of his life. He is the author of European art cinema masterpieces
Goto: Island of Love, Blanche and Immoral Tales, some surreal animated shorts, and controversial films such as The Beast. This new book concentrates on Borowczyk's feature
films, from Goto to Love Rites, which contain some of the most extraordinary images and
scenes in recent cinema. Erotica for some, porn for others, Borowczyk's films are highly
idiosyncratic and unforgettable.

Bibliography, notes, illustrations   240pp.
Paperback   ISBN 9781861712301   £15.00 / $30.00

Jean-Luc Godard

The Passion of Cinema /
Le Passion de Cinéma

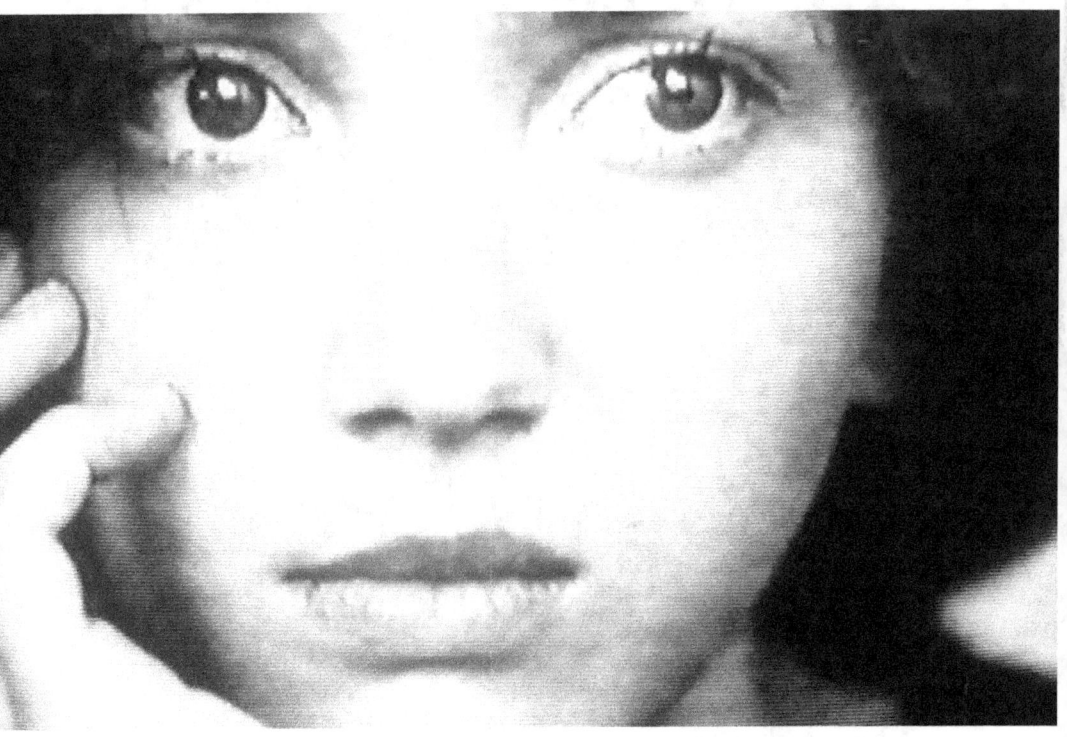

by Jeremy Mark Robinson

A new study of the French filmmaker Jean-Luc Godard (b. 1930),
director of iconic films such as *Breathless, Weekend, Pierrot le Fou,
Passion* and *Vivre Sa vie*. This book explores 27 of Godard's major films,
from *Breathless* to *Notre Musique*, and includes a scene by scene
analysis of Godard's controversial 1985 movie of the Virgin Mary,
Je Vous Salue, Marie.

Bibliography, notes, illustrations   420pp
Hardback   ISBN 9781761712271   £50.00 / $100.00

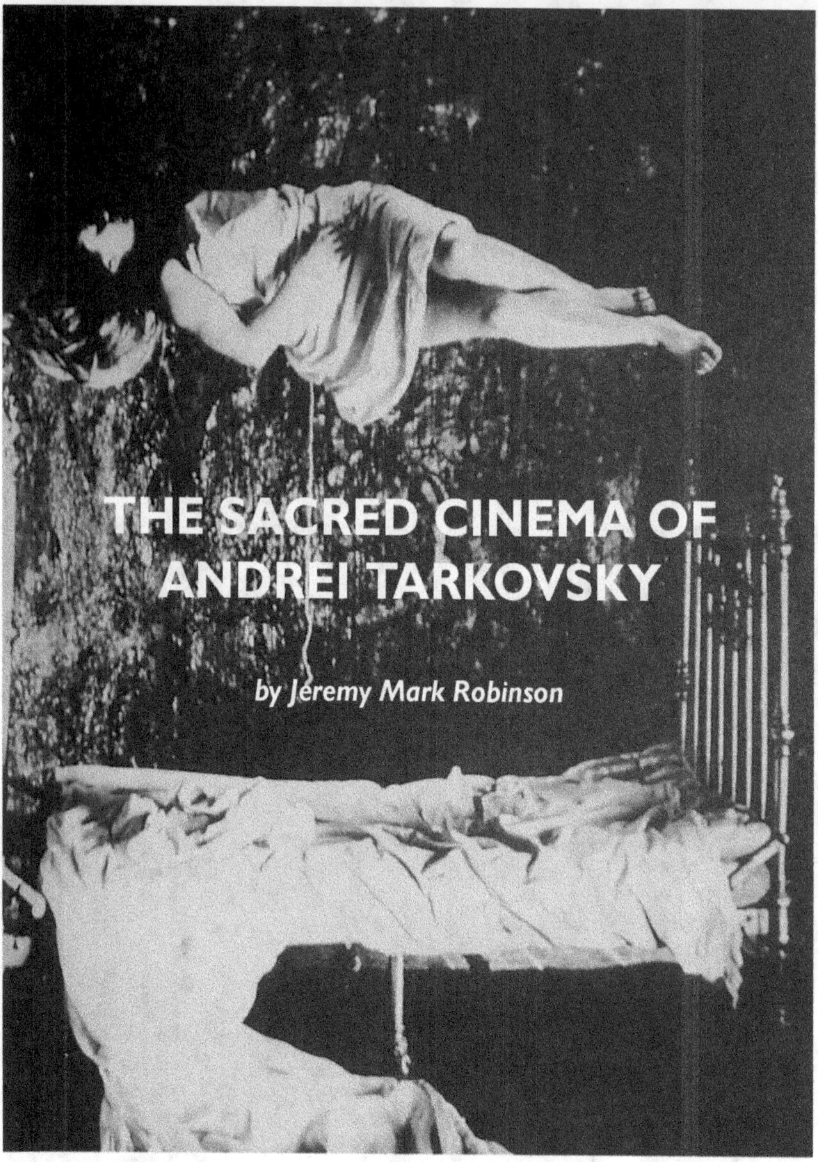

THE SACRED CINEMA OF
ANDREI TARKOVSKY

by Jeremy Mark Robinson

A new study of the Russian filmmaker Andrei Tarkovsky (1932-1986), director of seven feature films, including *Andrei Roublyov, Mirror, Solaris, Stalker* and *The Sacrifice*.

This is one of the most comprehensive and detailed studies of Tarkovsky's cinema available. Every film is explored in depth, with scene-by-scene analyses. All aspects of Tarkovsky's output are critiqued, including editing, camera, staging, script, budget, collaborations, production, sound, music, performance and spirituality. Tarkovsky is placed with a European New Wave tradition of filmmaking, alongside directors like Ingmar Bergman, Carl Theodor Dreyer, Pier Paolo Pasolini and Robert Bresson.

An essential addition to film studies.

Illustrations: 150 b/w, 4 colour. 682 pages. First edition. Hardback.

Publisher: Crescent Moon Publishing. Distributor: Gardners Books.

ISBN 1-86171-096-8 (9781861710963) £60.00 / $105.00

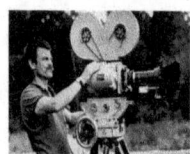

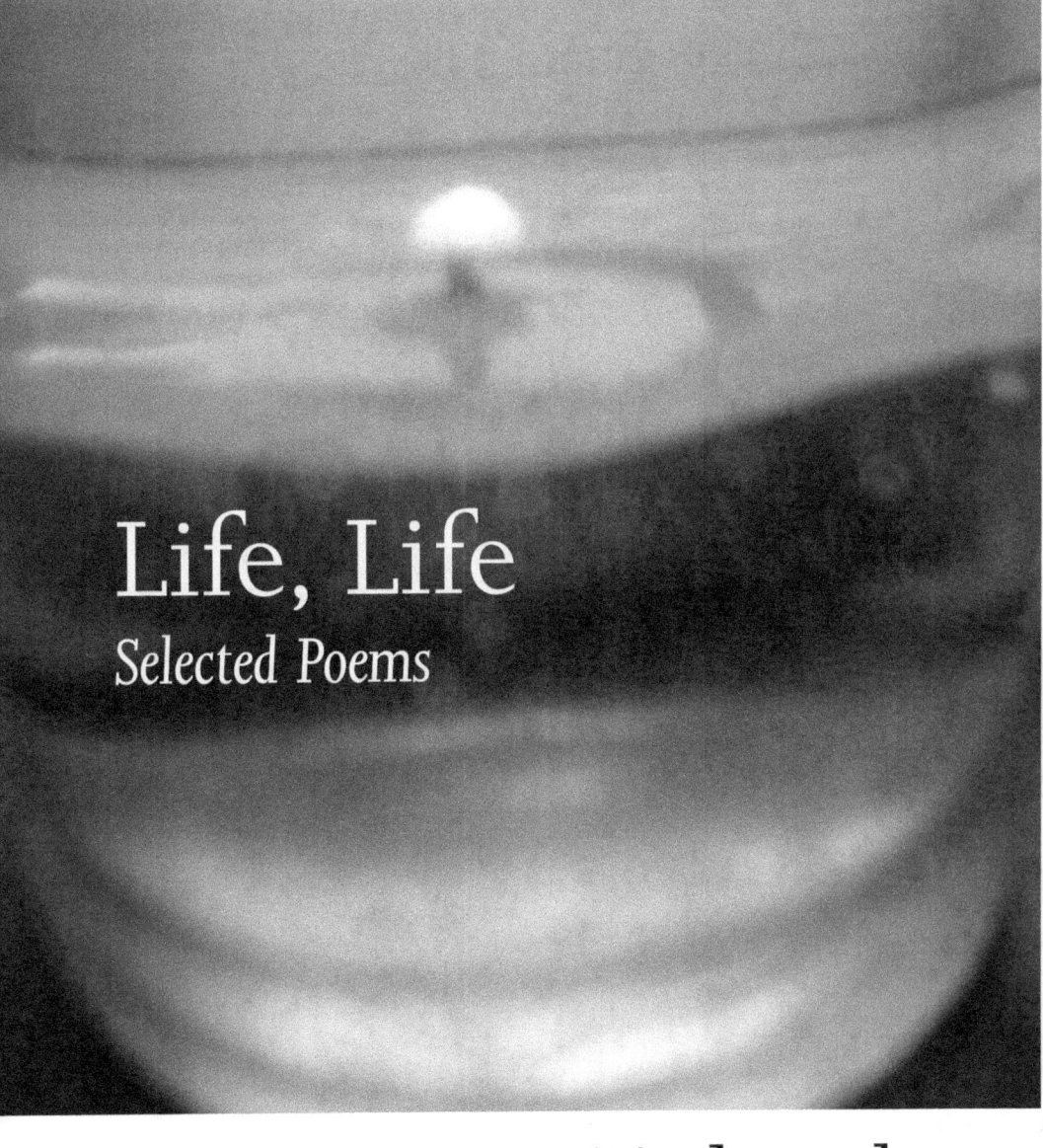

Life, Life
Selected Poems

Arseny Tarkovsky

translated and edited by Virginia Rounding

Arseny Tarkovsky is the neglected Russian poet, father of the acclaimed film director
Andrei Tarkovsky. This new book gathers together many of Tarkovsky's most lyrical
and heartfelt poems, in Rounding's clear, new translations. Many of Tarkovsky's poems
appeared in his son's films, such as *Mirror, Stalker, Nostalghia and The Sacrifice*.
There is an introduction by Rounding, and a bibliography of both Arseny and Andrei Tarkovsky.

Bibliography and notes   110pp   2nd ed   ISBN 1-86171-114-X   £10.00 / $20.00

In the Dim Void

Samuel Beckett's Late Trilogy:
Company, Ill Seen, Ill Said and *Worstward Ho*

by Gregory Johns

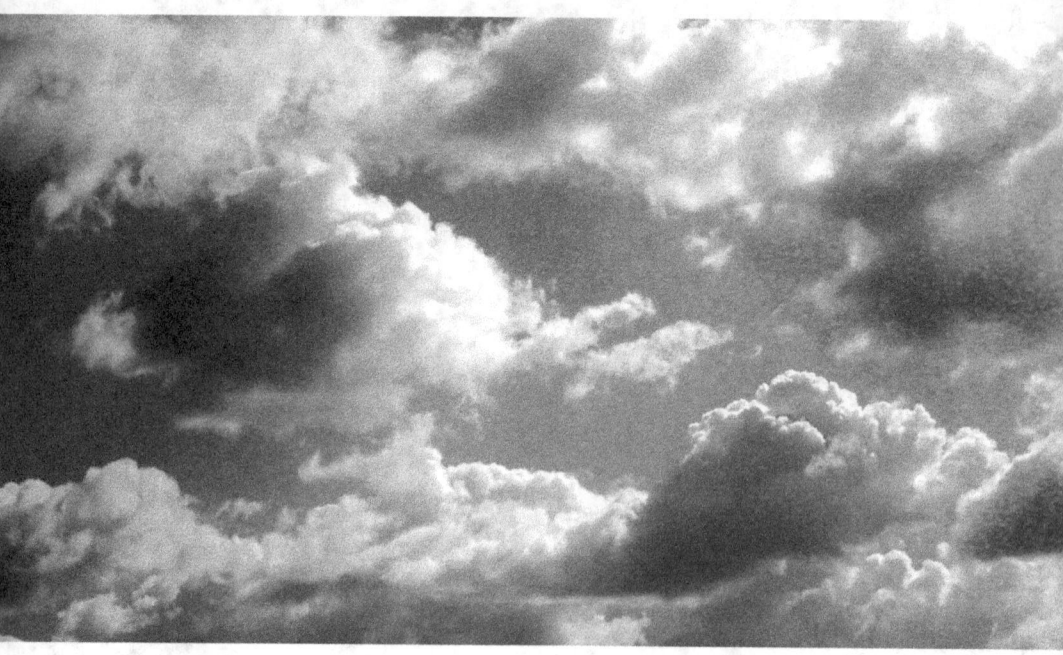

This book discusses the luminous beauty and dense, rigorous poetry of Beckett's late works, *Company, Ill Seen, Ill Said* and *Worstward Ho*. Johns looks back over Beckett's long writing career, charting the development from the *Molloy-Malone Dies-Unnamable* trilogy through the 'fizzles' of the 1960s to the elegiac lyricism of the *Company* series. Johns compares the trilogy with late plays such as *Ghosts, Footfalls* and *Rockaby*.

Bibliography, notes. 120pp
ISBN 1861710712 and ISBN 1861712356   £10.00 / $20.00

www.ingramcontent.com/pod-product-compliance
Lightning Source LLC
Chambersburg PA
CBHW071319220526
45468CB00001B/429